IT'S ALL ABOUT CHOICES

Lieutenant General Joseph S. Laposata (Retired)

DORRANCE
PUBLISHING CO
EST. 1920
PITTSBURGH, PENNSYLVANIA 15238

Dorrance Publishing Co
585 Alpha Drive
Suite 103
Pittsburgh, PA 15238
Visit our website at www.dorrancebookstore.com

ISBN: 978-1-4809-1256-4
eISBN: 978-1-4809-1578-7

CONTENTS

DEDICATION

This book is dedicated to my dear wife, Anita. Marrying her was like winning the lottery. She is smart, loving, kind and opinion-rich, with brilliant suggestions for the enrichment of my life.

It is also dedicated to the memory of my mother and father, Mary and Joseph Laposata, as well as my grandparents, Carmela and Michael Coco, and Violet and Samuel Laposata. I am eternally grateful for their loving and attentive parenting.

I am especially thankful to the United States Army. The Army provided me a moral and ethical environment in which to work. The officers, noncommissioned officers and soldiers I worked with were men and women of high character. I was frequently humbled by their absolute dedication to duty. Their example was my motivation to do my very best every day. I could not bring myself to fail these extraordinary American citizen soldiers.

I am also compelled to express my thanks to Judy Woods-Knight for her thorough review of the draft with recommendations for the improvement of my work. Thanks to the late Lilo Cross and Father Frank Simeone for their detailed readings of the manuscript. Gail Fay's attentive work in correcting all forms of grammar gone astray was notable. Douglas Guiler's keen and critical eye in matters of clarity, brevity and form reinforced the quality of the text. Finally, without Sharon Wilson's expert typing and administrative support, this effort would be relegated to oral history.

PREFACE

From the day I was born, my parents intentionally developed my life perspectives by providing me a broad range of character-building experiences while morally enhancing what talent I possessed prior to entering college. I was fortunate to be raised in a loving household by a father and mother, both grounded in church and family, who defined success as raising children with virtues and values. They believed in America as a unique land of opportunity. I embraced and sometimes just endured my parents' seventeen-year "character boot camp" while living under their roof. When the time came, I headed off to college, confident that I was both street and book smart. After four years of college, I noted that there were some members of my graduating class who were exceptionally talented and valued by the institution despite their high level of personal naiveté, lack of any practical experience and a severe shortfall of character. I wondered how they would fare when outside the protective cocoon of the school. It didn't take me long to find out.

Entering the Army as a 2nd lieutenant immediately upon graduation from college, I began to realize the value of my family's investment in my character. Talent, genius and education were broad and deep among my peers; they were very impressive young men. At first I thought that I was the least among them. I was too ethnic, had fewer social skills and had no network of Army friends. After my first assignment to an Infantry Brigade, I quickly realized that the Army did not care about my heritage, my religion or my family's social status. Of course, the Army wanted men and women who had talent and were educated; but it also wanted men and women of character who were persistent and determined to accomplish the mission while caring for the welfare of their troops. My family's credo was to work hard with dignity, take care of your family and your friends, be respectful of others and seek the positive side of daily life. When things turn sour, keep your focus and choose those options promoting the most positive outcomes. It sounded a lot like the Army's message. My parents' effort to develop my perspective as an "American child," intertwined with a foundation of Old World family wisdom, has served me well.

My father is identified as a principal source of wisdom and advice in the following short stories. I would be remiss if I left the impression that everything he said was a gem. Late in the evening on the day before I was to be married, my father approached me and said he wanted to share an important insight into married life. Up to this point he had been silent on the matter. I was understandably anxious to hear what he had to say. We retired to the kitchen and in a quiet but firm voice, looking me dead in the eye, he said, "Never learn to operate a household appliance." I was stunned to silence. "It can come to no good," he said. Standing even more erect, he continued, "Once you demonstrate your talent with the coffee machine, you will be performing on a regular basis." I suspect that in 1961, considering my father's Sicilian perspective on household management, he believed that what he said was sound advice. If I advanced that theory today, it would incite a homicide. My wife would kill me.

In the interest of truthful reporting, I must also report that my no-nonsense father went through a shocking metamorphosis when he became a grandfather. He offered little direction to his grandchildren but continued to give me advice on parenting; he was an easy touch for money and even took our kids for store bought pizza. I never heard him say to our boys, "When you go to college, be sure you study something that will get you a job." He was out of that business; he had served his watch. He made sure that I knew that it was my responsibility to pass the family wisdom to my children.

Realizing the brilliance of my family's wisdom encouraged me to catalog the stories of wisdom learned while I was still in my twenties. I have successfully used these stories to promote the concept of making proper choices for more than forty years. These vignettes have been employed for individual counseling as well as motivational and instructional lectures in military, governmental, diplomatic, commercial and academic venues. This text accumulates those stories addressing specific life management issues. They are straight-talking, take-away wisdom pertinent to everyday life issues.

The moral of the stories in this text are the important element to be grasped by the reader. The motives and actions of each individual portrayed are equally meaningful. The real life identity of the individuals and the location of the stories are irrelevant. I have done my utmost to masquerade people and places.

There are very few entries in this text that contain elements of my personal wisdom. I was not given the gift of profound thought. I was, however, given the gift of observation and the ability to retain and replicate the wisdom of others. I have done my best to give credit where credit is due.

Some may read these stories and believe they are an exercise of my ego since I am the functional character in each story. It is with some reluctance that I bare my soul on my adolescent escapades but my parents' wisdom is demonstrated through my own faults and shortcomings.

I am hopeful that I have captured the love and caring nature of my family. To some the lessons may seem to be of the "tough love" variety, but the operative word here is "love." There was never a denigrating, physically abusive or emotionally punitive aspect to their approach. My family simply ensured that I understood the lesson to be learned.

I am not a psychiatrist, a social scientist or a minister and these stories are not based on academic human relations theory. Rather, the stories illustrate wisdom hardened by the fire of trial and error over many generations. These stories are the precious knowledge of men and women who for generations have made the right choices; the choices that permitted them to adapt, to survive, to prosper, to love and be happy. This wisdom has been given to me and I am sharing it with you.

I CAN SEE FARTHER THAN MY FATHER
BECAUSE I AM STANDING ON MY
FATHER'S SHOULDERS
Arab Proverb

NOTHING IN THE WORLD
CAN TAKE THE PLACE
OF PERSISTENCE.
TALENT WILL NOT;
NOTHING IS MORE COMMON THAN
UNSUCCESSFUL MEN WITH TALENT.
GENIUS WILL NOT;
UNREWARDED GENIUS
IS ALMOST A PROVERB.
EDUCATION WILL NOT;
THE WORLD IS FULL
OF EDUCATED DERELICTS.
PERSISTENCE AND DETERMINATION
ALONE ARE OMNIPOTENT.

Calvin Coolidge,
Thirtieth President of the United States.

CHAPTER ONE

WISDOM OF THE ELDERS

It's All About Choices

Positive life experiences are usually the outcome of using good judgment in making choices. Good judgment must be learned; it is not an inherited trait. Families, institutions and our culture must strive to teach, demonstrate and promote the wisdom essential for developing good judgment in our children. Otherwise, they will be relegated to tolerating the pain of learning from their failures caused by making poor choices resulting from bad judgment.

Life enrichment books are a staple in most bookstores. However, it seems a requirement for the authors of many of these books to experience a messy divorce, alcohol or drug abuse, clinical depression or some other life altering experience before personal enrichment could occur. One author even stated that she *had* to "screw up" her life just to find a better way to live. She was over 40 years old when she discovered the link between making proper choices and achieving happiness. The woman was deeply regretful at having wasted half of her life on poor choices, bad judgment and dreadful personal experiences.

In truth, there is nothing new in that woman's story. When I was in my late teens, a wise, old, Italian immigrant friend of my father advised me that positive life experiences were usually the outcome of making sound moral and ethical choices. He went on to add that making wise and virtuous choices was based on a foundation of good judgment resident in one's character. Good judgment, he said, is not inherited; it is developed by accepting, understanding and employing the wisdom passed by one's elders; in this case, my parents. Good judgment was something to be learned, he said. Then with some sadness in his voice, he noted that good judgment also has roots in living through a bad experience. That is, one may learn from the negative experience of a bad situation. Significantly, the bad situation was usually the product of poor judgment. His punch line was that I should make it a point to listen to my father's wisdom and build a foundation of good judgment in my character. He also advised me that judgment improves with practice and that I should regularly, but silently and internally, assess the judgments of others. Observing the outcomes of choices made by friends and then asking myself what would I have done differently was a very constructive piece of advice. It really helped me develop my judgmental skills.

My father made certain I clearly understood the difference between knowledge and wisdom. Knowledge, he said, was an understanding gained through experience or study and that was why my attendance at a college was essential. However, just being book smart was not enough. Wisdom, on the other hand, was an understanding of what is true, proper and right, and that was something I was to learn from my family through observation, experience and attention to their stories. In short, wisdom was the key to maximizing the proper application of my knowledge. He used a line that he heard somewhere to drive this point home. "Knowledge," he said, "is knowing that the tomato is a fruit. Wisdom is not putting tomatoes into a fruit salad."

The wisdom of my parents was conveyed to me in a litany of lessons passed in a stream of discerning micro bytes of information intended to expose the negative and reinforce the positive aspects of life's issues. Their basic theme was that life is all about the choices we make in our daily lives. In matters of self-discipline, integrity, judgment, initiative and moral courage, the choices we make are the difference in the quality of our lives.

Following their guidance, my professional life has been rewarding and my personal life has been filled with joy and contentment. Stress, depression and anxiety have rarely been my companions. I married a young woman who shared and reinforced my perspective on making proper choices. Being of one mind on these fundamental issues enhanced our relationship and we grew together, loving and managing our family.

The wisdom of my parents' child rearing theory was passed to them by their parents. They made certain I knew the origin of their developmental strategy for me and my siblings. Our family came to the United States so that my generation would secure the opportunity to be all that it could be. My father's generation was devoted to firmly establishing the businesses founded by my grandparents in America. That stabilizing effort was to be the springboard for my generation to achieve status as university professors, medical doctors, business executives and officers in the Armed Forces. I knew the immigrants well and listened to their stories about the "old country." I felt it a responsibility not to disappoint but rather to confirm their belief in the opportunity and goodness of life in the United States by meeting their expectations as an "American child."

My father often repeated the family's two-part perspective on raising children. First, I was to *learn* about life's realities while living under their roof. They openly addressed moral and immoral behavior in all its forms. The good and bad of the human condition was an ongoing discussion in our home.

They also believed that there was a reason for everything that happened. When something unpleasant occurred in my life it was my responsibility to refrain from whining and complaining about the situation. I was assured that some of the things that I initially might have believed were negative impacts on my life would, in the long run, produce fortuitous outcomes.

Secondly, they knew that if I chose to employ their wisdom, I would be better prepared to live my adult life with confidence after learning to manage life's less pleasant matters while living under their protective umbrella. I was not to be a sheltered child. It was all about *using* the wisdom *learned* from my family to make *judicious* choices for the remainder of my life.

My father believed that there was a definable inventory of poor choices to be made in the average person's life. The issue was not whether these mistakes would be made, but when in life's timeline they would occur. He advised that the worst of all cases was to have these mistakes occur as an adult. The punitive effects of poor choices at that point in life produce the deepest emotional scars and usually have a longer recovery period. My parents were determined that my adult life would not be an on-the-job learning experience. As a result, they did a marvelous job in preparing me to deal with joy and sorrow, industry and indolence, accomplishment and failure.

Life is all about making proper choices. You cannot outsource choice management. Take responsibility and accountability for your choices. It is never too late to start.

CHAPTER TWO

TESTA DURA

Self-discipline is the Foundation of Character

That voice we hear in our brain advising us to "do the right thing" is often in conflict with yet another voice recommending just the opposite. Making the proper choice is often a more difficult road to travel, but having the self-discipline to do the right thing produces outcomes that will enrich your life and often the lives of others. Choose to follow the suggestions of that other voice and sooner than later, you will pay the price for that moment of self-indiscipline and poor judgment.

My father often noted that until I was sixteen years old, I thought my name was Testa Dura. It was one of his favorite names for me. Literally translated from the Italian language as "hard head," it goes a bit further in meaning. To be a card-carrying Testa Dura, one must, of course, be donkey stubborn. Couple that with a tendency to act before thinking and Testa Dura is a name earned, not bestowed. In short, self-discipline was not one of my adolescent strong points.

My father had a special gift of common sense and logic. He was the man called to mediate when friends or family members were at odds. My father could always find some middle ground, satisfy both parties, without prejudice, and work out a settlement. The man could bring order out of chaos. His words and wisdom were respected because his moral self-discipline to do what was right, good and proper was unquestioned. He wanted the insight of common sense and logic for me but my lack of self-discipline smothered the gift.

The issue, according to my dad, was my unbridled enthusiasm. I didn't do anything really bad as a youngster; I never had a police record and was not in trouble at school. My transgressions fell into the category of "How in heaven's name did you come up with an idea like that?"

For example, after third grade summer school catechism class, a kid "double dared" me to wade across the Conemaugh River. This is the same river that the great Johnstown Flood followed into the city in 1889 and killed 2,209 people. The kid said that the river was haunted and that anyone trespassing its bed would be dragged under and drowned. "The river," he reported, "had tasted death, liked it, and wanted more." It was a scary story, but it was early summer and the river was at low ebb. It quickly came to me that with a little luck one could walk on the large stones above the water line part way across and wade the last few yards. I thought the kid's story did not meet the common sense test and I was prepared to challenge the ghosts. I had my younger brother, Sammy, with me, and I convinced him that he should cross with me, acting as my assistant. I confess that my intentions were not entirely honorable. Logic assured me that if I went alone and there was some truth to the "evil river spirit" theory, I was a goner. If Sammy came along, the evil ghosts had a choice of kids to devour, and my odds of crossing safely improved significantly.

With a group of kids standing on the river wall watching our every move, we went wading. Of course, we made it to the other side with only damp clothes to show for the crossing. I was a hero to my classmates and so was my first-grade, ghost-bait assistant. We had disproved the "evil river spirit" theory. The double-daring kid was exposed as a fraud and he went home sulking. That's the good news. The bad news is that his mother and my mother were friends. When the kid arrived home late, his mother asked where he had been. He told her the details of our river crossing adventure, omitting the part about the double dare, and she couldn't wait to call my mother. I can still see the fear in my mother's face when she confronted me wanting the details of our river crossing adventure.

I was less than cooperative about answering my mother's direct line of questioning, so she turned to Sammy. He broke on the first question. Sammy told the story about the double dare, his supporting role as my assistant, and holding his shoes over his head as he waded to the riverbank. The more he talked, the deeper the hole I was in. My only defense was that I believed that we had an obligation to disprove the kid's stupid story about the "haunted" river. No one was buying my story. Who knew that the kid would tell his mother and that Sammy would "cough up" the truth the first time he was squeezed? Frankly, it never dawned on me that the crossing was dangerous and that responding to the double dare was less than brilliant. My lack of self-discipline in responding to the double dare and my refusal to accept responsibility for the river crossing (I wouldn't have done it if the kid hadn't issued the double dare) put me in parental hot water.

About a year after the river incident, a friend and I were hiking with a group to a fire tower in a nearby forest. We were to have a lunch at the tower and return home early in the afternoon. While the group settled in to eat their sandwiches at the tower, we spotted a deer at the edge of the forest. My friend and I quietly abandoned the group to follow the deer and in the process, became disoriented in the forest on Laurel Mountain. At that point, we were over four hours late coming home. In a few hours it would be dark. We got our bearings when we found a stream plummeting down the mountain into the valley. The stream led to a dam and a cabin inhabited by an old man. As we approached, he came out of his cabin carrying a shotgun. He asked us, in a not-too-friendly tone, what we were doing on his property.

We told him the story of the deer, that we were lost and had followed the stream to his place. He asked us our names and went inside the cabin and called the local chapter of the Pennsylvania State Police to come get us.

The state policeman finally arrived, traveling up the dirt trail leading to and ending at the old man's cabin. He contacted my worried parents through a radio-telephone link up. The state cop talked the old guy into dropping his charge of trespassing and we were out of there.

Riding in the high-tech police car was exciting. When we got to the highway, he headed like lightning toward Johnstown with his alert lights blinking. "Wow," I thought to myself, "it just doesn't get better than this."

The cop was a big guy, impeccably dressed. He quickly informed us that this rescue operation was hindering his ability to catch crooks and other evildoers. "This better not happen again," he said. We promised, sincerely, that he would never see us in his car again, ever.

When we arrived at my home there were many people waiting for us. My mother was crying, and she embraced me in front of everyone kissing me all over my face. She was going from the emotion of "frantic" to one of "relief." My father had long passed through "frantic" and "relief" and was now firmly rooted in "anger."

When I told my dad the story about not staying with the group and deciding to follow the deer, he could only mutter, "What in God's name were you thinking?" According to my father, I made a poor choice to follow the deer, but it was my lack of self-discipline to follow instructions and to stay with the group that was at the root of the issue. The Testa Dura legend was growing.

My mother could successfully keep my dad at bay when I failed by noting that I was "just a child." She was my advocate and she could manipulate my father in my favor. Mom was my personal lawyer.

Things were a little strained at home for the next few days, yet I reveled in the dubious honor of having a ride in a State Police car without having been handcuffed in the process. Well, at least the guys who hung around our corner thought it was cool.

The incident that broke the camel's back occurred later that summer. Finding a streetcar token awakened my intense desire to travel. It was through a simple misunderstanding concerning trolley transfer slips that left a friend and me stranded at the end of the trolley line in Franklin, Pennsylvania. I had heard about Franklin, located on the outskirts of Johnstown, and thought it was a place I should see. When the conductor informed us that transfer slips were not issued at the end of the line for a ride back to the city, we were reduced to panhandling waiting passengers for the ten cents to get us back home. Luck was not with us until my friend began to cry. He claimed it was just an act; it was an act that encouraged a nice man to give us the dime, but not before he asked us our names. It turns out he knew my mother's family and mentioned my "Franklin adventure" to one of my uncles. My dear uncle returned the ten cents to the gentleman and passed the story to my mother.

I deliberately chose not to tell my parents of the trolley ride to Franklin. I really didn't think it was all that important.

After my parents heard the details of the story, Mom, being very concerned, asked if this event was an attempt to run away from home. That sort of thing was in vogue with some kids at the time. I assured them I was quite happy; it's just that I had an opportunity to "travel" and decided not to let the opportunity pass me by. The logic of that statement escaped my parents and compelled them to joint action.

This episode diminished my mother's previously unwavering support and protection. My father took the lead in managing my self-discipline issues. At a family meeting, with my grandparents present, he announced that I had too many ideas, I was lacking the self-discipline to sort them out and I was not taking responsibility for my ill-conceived actions. All concurred that the time was ripe to take immediate and direct action. I knew something was going to change; I just didn't know how much and when.

Dad decided that I was to begin my metamorphosis by securing an appreciation of the work ethic. Proceeding on the theory that "idle hands were the devil's tools," I was put to work at age ten sweeping the sidewalk in front of the barbershop, convenience store, and beauty shop that my father owned. I was also appointed the barbershop janitor.

To insure a clean shop and sidewalk first thing in the morning it was necessary to tidy them up at the close of business. During the first week of cleanup duty, I chose to hang out with friends at the corner one evening rather than clean the shop and sweep the sidewalk. I figured I would do it later. Arriving home and wanting to sleep, I chose to set the alarm clock and get up early to do the job before the shop opened. When the alarm rang, half groggy and not remembering the last evening's intent for an early cleaning detail, I shut it off and went back to sleep. My dad noted my "dereliction of duty" as he opened the shop in the morning. Without an evil word, he got me out of bed and had me clean up the shop and sweep the sidewalk in front

of customers and passersby while wearing slippers and pajamas. It only happened once.

My father's insistence on my having the self-discipline
to think before acting did not quickly penetrate my intellect.
Self-discipline did not come easy to me; according to my
wife, I'm still working on it.

My parents believed that character was built on a foundation of self-discipline. They considered it the essential
human software required to properly download and install
the other elements of character. Consequently, beginning at
age ten, my life became a series of lessons intended to instill
in me a sense of self-discipline. There was a moral to every
lesson and my parents made certain I understood the moral
of the story. Notably, when my mother became a member
of the prosecution, change was around the corner. Her kind,
loving and nurturing style combined with my father's no-
nonsense, unemotional, business-like approach quickly
turned on some lights in my head.

Less than brilliant choices and the resulting regrettable
outcomes were not an option in our home. Fortunately, my
parents' logical, affectionate but firm approach in defining
my failure worked well with me. I did not respond to threats
or angry voices inside or outside the home.

Their persistence and determination to encourage me to
a higher level of self-discipline was admirable. Once I got the
idea my life became a happier affair. I may not have enjoyed
the extended process of learning this lesson, but it margin-
alized anxiety, insecurity, and stress in my adult life.

Choose to manage your self-discipline; it really is the
foundation of a strong character. It's an offer you can't afford to refuse.

Chapter Three

Gary Was a World Class Liar

The Lack Of Integrity Cannot Be Concealed Or Condoned

On occasion we find an individual who is absolutely devoid of integrity. Lying, cheating and stealing are a way of life for these folks. They are dangerous to well-functioning organizations as they cannot be counted upon to subscribe to an established code of moral behavior. Mutual trust and confidence in all members of an organization is essential if it is to function efficiently and effectively. Expose these individuals and their irresponsible behavior to the proper authority; do not tolerate their disease as it will destroy individuals and organizations.

My parents were intent on insuring that their children spoke the truth, the whole truth and nothing but the truth on a daily basis with no exceptions. While I do not recall any specific issues about which I lied as a four year old, my mother told me that my inclination at that age was never to tell the truth when a lie would serve me just as well. I do recall a corner in our kitchen that was called "Purgatory." I was required to stand in silence in "Purgatory" facing the wall after being caught telling a falsehood. This was never a pleasant affair. By the time I started the first grade I had spent sufficient time in "Purgatory" to clearly understand the value of always telling the truth. Notably, the "Purgatory" drill ingrained in me the need to meet my parents' standards for speaking the truth even when guilty of an offense. Throwing myself on the mercy of the family court was far better than doing time in the Purgatory slammer.

I never had a cheating incident as a youngster and I was uninformed of that dysfunctional behavior except by observing it in others. Cheating was an option in my life at school, but when I considered the embarrassment it would bring to my parents if I were found out, I decided that I could not cheat; I could not hurt those people who were so dear to me. To possibly bring shame or embarrassment to my family was an option I could not exercise.

The Ten Commandments were baseline directives in my family. As a child, a full understanding of some of the Ten Commandments was obscure, but the "Do Not Steal" directive was easy to understand and my father especially made that Commandment one of his teaching points. Lying, cheating and stealing were big time violations of our family's code of conduct. They made certain that I understood that guidance. I still marvel at the wisdom of my parents shaping my intellect as a child to live a simple, anxiety free life by following just a few basic rules of positive human behavior.

Fast forwarding now to the late 1950s, I attended a Reserve Officers Training Corps (ROTC) six-week training camp during the summer. I had spoken with friends who had attended this camp before me and I was like a loaded pistol when I arrived for the training. I knew what to do, when to do it and how to do it. My friends had prepared me well for the experience of ROTC Summer Camp. Assigned a bunk in a World War II era barracks of forty cadets and two Regular Army Sergeants, I set out immediately cleaning my area, preparing a footlocker to specification and doing only enough socializing to introduce myself.

After a day of orientation we were told that we would stand our initial inspection the next morning. Written instructions for the inspection were passed out and we worked into the night to prepare. Well, almost everyone worked into the night. A cadet named Gary was a student at a private military school. He advised one and all that he knew the inspection routine and that he was not going to be pushed around by any lieutenant or sergeant. While we were working to spit shine everything in sight he sat on his unmade bunk eating chips and drinking a soda. He was a funny guy, had a super personality and entertained us with interesting stories. In short order he accumulated a few disciples. He put them to work shining his shoes and cleaning his equipment. As they were finishing up, one of his flunkies accidentally spilled chocolate milk on Gary's blanket and it left a large stain. As they were discussing what to do with the blanket, the lights were turned out and we were told to sleep.

At the inspection the next day, Gary made his bed with the stain predominately displayed for the inspecting officer. When he was asked about the stain, his response was immediate and assured. He told the lieutenant that the blanket had been issued to him in that condition and that when he tried to exchange it the supply room had closed. He was very sorry that he was not fully prepared for the inspection but this matter was beyond his control. The lieutenant bought his story and Gary passed the inspection with minor demerits. His lie was delivered so flawlessly even those of us who knew what happened were impressed. He delivered a few more lies over the next few weeks to avoid work or to cover up his shortfalls, always depending on his flunkies and the rest of the platoon to remain silent. He even delivered a short speech on how "stoolies" were treated at his military college. No one wanted to be a "stoolie."

During our first exam I noticed Gary and one of his flunkies cheating. Gary may have been a charming personality and an entertainer, but in truth he was rather stupid. His scores were always just above passing. There was not a chance he would be competing for the Outstanding Cadet Award. I was a witness to Gary's lying, cheating and butt kissing. I was amazed how a slick talking guy with a handsome face, attending a prestigious school could get away with so much while the rest of us were held to toeing the line. We had a fellow cadet, nicknamed "Fumbles," who was bright, loved the Army, was small in stature and worked harder than everyone else just to keep up with the physical requirements of the training. He and Gary were not on the best of terms as Gary frequently picked on him because of his lack of physical coordination; in short, "Fumbles" was a klutz.

After completing a Land Navigation exercise on a very hot day we were all short of water in our canteens. Notably, the resupply truck was nowhere to be seen. Gary and his boys were soliciting water from others with little success. When he came to "Fumbles," who was exhausted and prudently sipping water from his canteen, Gary snatched the canteen from "Fumbles" hand and gulped a few big swigs. "Fumbles" had had enough of Gary and a pushing match ensued. It was an uneven match and "Fumbles" ended up on his back with Gary's boot on his chest. Order was restored as the resupply truck arrived and everyone lined up for water. It was quite clear to me that Gary's behavior was becoming less amusing and more debilitating to the platoon.

While I didn't want to be a stoolie, it was time to have Gary, the platoon informal leader, account for his stewardship. He never bothered me as I was a quiet, serious person with a few good buddies who could sweep the floor with Gary. After our platoon did poorly on a field training exercise that was due in large part to the dysfunctional relationship among the platoon members, we were compelled to repeat the exercise while the rest of the company was having dinner. I was appointed the new platoon leader. My first act was to isolate Gary and his thugs with an assignment as flank security, and the platoon pulled off the drill with precision. When we went to dinner the Cadre Company Commander invited me to eat at his table with the officers. Of course, they wanted to know how I motivated the platoon to perform so well so quickly.

I told them that the unit was motivated to do well because I removed those cadets who were not motivated. The company commander asked me what that meant. I advised him that I was not a "stoolie." However, if he wanted to talk about it man-to-man, on a professional basis, I would relate my perspectives as objectively as I could. The next morning after Physical Training, a runner came to our platoon asking me to report to the Company Commander. He had my cadre lieutenant in his office and he asked me what I meant by removing the unmotivated.

I gave him my perspective and related events as they occurred from the first day of camp relating to Gary. When I was finished, the company commander advised me that I was not a "stoolie" and that it was my obligation not to tolerate those who would lie, cheat or steal. He said I should be proud that I came forward because the Army would not tolerate that kind of behavior in its officers. I left the company commander's office regretful that I had not done something sooner about Gary's fractious character. I vowed I would never be reluctant in the future to deal with character-deficient personalities like Gary.

Somehow Gary received a commission and entered the active Army. I was serving in Germany two years later and noted in the newspaper that an officer had been court martialed for misuse of his Unit Fund and selling government property. You guessed it, the person going to jail and being booted out of the Army was our boy Gary. If only Gary's mother had a "Purgatory Corner" perhaps the Army could have been saved from the embarrassment he brought to this marvelous organization.

I learned a lot from Gary. I learned what not to do. I also worked for one fellow some years later who was also morally shy. Once again I was enriched by observing his behavior and performance as something that I never wanted to do. Even if tempted to join up and emulate his behavior, how would I ever be able to tell my parents of a character shortfall that might result in my dismissal from the Army? The point to be made here is that, even when in the presence of those who are morally benign, the issue of integrity can be reinforced.

Integrity is one of the essential elements of honorable character. There will be times in your life when it seems that those with less integrity are prospering. Be persistent and determined to retain your personal and professional integrity as men and women of integrity will rise to the top in the long run. If you are integrity deficient you will be found out. If you seek honor and achievement, your personal integrity must be intact 24/7.

CHAPTER FOUR

THE RED RACER

Understanding Guidance and Avoiding Assumptions

Conflicting guidance from multiple sources is to be avoided. When one is given a task, it is imperative that the person giving the task and the person receiving the guidance have a perfect understanding as to the who, what, when, where, why and how the task is to be completed. Failure and discord are guaranteed if all parties are not operating from the same set of expectations. Ask questions if you don't fully understand guidance. Success becomes the predominant outcome when tasks are properly coordinated.

Every summer when I was a young boy my maternal grandparents, Mike and Carmela Coco, rented a cottage in the country. It was along a creek large enough for swimming and the fish were plentiful. Time spent there with my grandparents constitutes some of my most cherished childhood memories.

When I was six or seven years old and staying at the cottage with my grandparents, my grandfather announced that he was going to Harrisburg, Pennsylvania for a meeting and that he would remain for an extra day to visit a friend. He asked if I would like to go with him. Of course I said, "Yes." There was nothing like an adventure with my grandfather.

Arriving in the big city, we stayed with my grandfather's friend and his family. Heeding my grandfather's admonition to "be a good boy," I was on my best behavior.

While my grandfather was at his meeting, I hung out in our host's grocery store, watching and speaking with customers. As a child, socializing with customers in our family businesses was my delight. I enjoyed their conversations, debates, and stories. I quickly found that the folks in the great metropolis of Harrisburg were no different from those in our much smaller hometown. They were pleasant and liked to chat with an outgoing little kid.

There was a dinner at a hotel on the second evening of my grandfather's meeting and I went with him. I was uncertain about what was going to take place and what I was to do. When I inquired, my grandfather said, "Act like I do, use your best manners and speak to others like you speak to me." That guidance was clear; I knew exactly what he wanted me to do.

My grandfather and I worked the room, shaking hands and speaking with people at almost every table. Other men had children with them. One child was crying, a few were misbehaving, and some were shy. At my grandfather's side, I confidently acted like a little Mike Coco. We sat for dinner and listened to a speech. When it was over, we were among the last to leave.

I knew I had done well, but my grandfather said nothing when I was put to bed. The next day we went shopping for a gift for my grandmother. Coming to a toy store, he said, "Let's go in and see what they have for a good boy." My mother and father were well aware of my grandfather's generosity toward my brother and me, so they had given me specific guidance to accept only something small and inexpensive if he insisted on a gift.

It took me a while to go through the store, as every shelf seemed to have something more enticing than the last. My parents' words of fiscal prudence were resounding in my head. The dilemma was more than I could deal with, so, in an act of desperation, I finally selected a small balsa wood airplane that could be made to fly by sliding the wings and tail through slots in the fuselage.

To say the least, my grandfather was shocked. He asked me if the airplane was what I really wanted. I then told him of my parents' admonition about selecting a small gift. He knelt down on one knee and looking me straight in the eye, spoke directly to me. "When you are with me, my rules, not your parents' rules are in effect. Don't worry about getting into trouble, as I'll take care of them. Remember, your mother is my daughter, and she will listen to me."

Never having thought about it that way, I saw the logic in his words. He then said, "If you buy that wooden airplane, it will break in a few days and you will not have anything later on in life that will remind you of our time together in Harrisburg. Now, let's look again and do it by my rules."

Earlier, I had seen a red racing car that was super, but rejected it because I was certain it cost too much. When I took my grandfather to the Red Racer he said, "This is perfect. It will last a long time and someday, if you are careful with it, you will look at it and think of this special time we had together." When we returned home, my parents were not upset about the purchase of the Red Racer. My dad thought it was a neat gift and played with me, pushing the Red Racer back and forth on the street in front of our home.

I was always encouraged to ask questions if I did not completely understand what I was told to do. My parents could understand failure to complete a task successfully. It is an imperfect world and things like that happen. However, they refused to accept failure when it was the result of my not understanding guidance. This lesson stuck to me like Velcro. I always made it a point to be certain I was on the same sheet of music with the person who was giving me a task.

As a young Army officer, when I was given a task, I was equally determined to fully understand my boss's guidance. I never felt embarrassed to ask a question to better understand what had to be done. Failure, in some cases, was a guarantee if I just accepted direction and ran with it. I always made certain the boss knew I was not questioning his authority. Simply, I was determined that we both knew what was wanted.

When I began giving the direction, I much preferred and even encouraged people to ask me questions to clarify the tasks I wanted accomplished. It often helped me give better direction, and I was assured of their understanding. When giving guidance, if no questions were forthcoming I often would ask, "Now, tell me back what I just told you."

The few minutes spent to become of one mind on an issue saved hours of time redirecting an errant understanding of my intent or dealing with a failure. The home and the workplace are also more efficient and happier places when all parties are working from the same baseline.

It is equally important to be of steady emotion when discussing guidance. Emotions have a way of impairing the auditory function and accompanying mental processes. Everything takes longer when emotions are blooming.

Now, when I look at the Red Racer in my office, I often think of my grandfather and his wisdom: Understand what is expected of you and work to satisfy *one* set of expectations. If you do not fully understand or want to be certain that you know precisely what you are required to do, respectfully ask for guidance. In short, understand the game before you begin to play. If you are faced with conflicting guidance from more than one source, get it cleared up quickly. Accounting for your stewardship to multiple sources of conflicting guidance guarantees failure.

Stress is guaranteed when uncertainty is in play. If you are unsure of what to accomplish, anxiety will be your constant companion. You may be stressed out over the magnitude or complexity of the task, but that is a different matter.

A person may have talent, genius and education, but if that individual fails to secure clear guidance before setting out to accomplish a task, the probability of success in dealing with that issue is in doubt. ATTENTION: Be advised that assumptions are road blocks to success and are to be avoided. The old Army line about assumptions is that when you "assume," there is a good chance that you will make an ASS out of U and ME.

Assuming you know what the boss wants done is often the first step on a slippery slope leading to failure. Focus on getting the job done right, the first time. It is a choice that will illuminate your performance, highlight your potential and set you apart from your peers.

Chapter Five

Somebody Stole My Pencil Box

Take the Initiative

Initiative has been studied in detail at academic institutions. However, to keep it simple and expand the perspective of initiative, be assured that if initiative is not managed, if it is not focused, if it is not directed, initiative will consume individuals and material resources with few positive outcomes. Poorly managed initiatives will destroy competent individuals, mighty institutions and sagacious ideas. History is replete with examples.

I was one of those kids who couldn't wait to enter the first grade. My mother started working with me a year before I entered school on phonetic reading exercises and my father taught me simple math. When the first day of school drew near, we purchased some clothes for the school year. My dear grandmother insisted that I have a modest but colorful pencil box to complete my kit. It held four pencils and an eraser in the lid. With the pencil box in hand, my mother walked me to school that first day. She confirmed my classroom and teacher's name, took me to the classroom door, kissed me and she was gone. I had no feeling of separation or isolation; I just wanted to get on with it. I could *do* this reading and math stuff and I couldn't wait to *show* somebody what I knew.

The student desks were arranged in the room in three clusters. The grouping on the far right of the room had a sign noting that they were the "Lions." The teacher began to call names and filled the seats in that grouping. My name was not called. The center grouping of students was under a sign that said "Eagles." Those seats were quickly filled by the teacher; notably, my name was not called to be an Eagle. On the far left of the room the sign in front of that grouping of desks was titled "Busy Bees." There were only eight kids left to be seated. One was of Greek heritage, another was Jewish, a couple of Slavic heritage kids, two poor kids, another boy of Italian origin and me. When we were assigned our seats I was the last to be seated. I had played pick up baseball in my neighborhood and knew that the last kid to be selected was usually perceived to be a "loser" and I suspected that was the teacher's perception of me.

Just to confirm things, the Italian kid seated in front of me turned around and said, "*Paisano*, my name is Carlo." (*Paisano* is roughly translated as someone who shares an Italian heritage.) "I was in this class last year and flunked first grade. I sat in your seat last year and that seat is reserved for the dumbest kid in the class. At least I'm starting out better this year." I was five years old, skinny, small and very serious. That combination got me awarded with the class dunce desk. I was not happy with the assignment but sat there intent on doing my best. The teacher was kind and presented the rules for the classroom. Suddenly a bell rang notifying the teacher that we were to be released to the school grounds for recess. I had been holding my prized pencil box in my hand since walking into the room. The teacher told us to leave anything we had with us on our desk and line up for recess. I followed Carlo out to the playground and stayed with him as he knew his way around. We even went to talk to some second graders who had been his classmates last year.

When we returned to the classroom, I immediately went to my desk to retrieve my pencil box. It was gone! I frantically looked through my desk, and checked the floor. I asked Carlo if he had seen it and, in an act of desperation, stood up and without asking permission to speak, blurted out in a teary voice that someone had stolen my pencil box while we were at recess. The teacher had been down this road before. She immediately went into the detective mode. The questions came fast, her face was not a happy one and she truly believed I was lying... After all, I *was* an "Italian." I think she thought I had sold or traded it and was looking for a cover story. I had been in school only two hours, the pencil box was gone and the teacher was not an ally. I was not off to a good start. I walked home for lunch but I did not bring up the issue of the missing pencil box. My mother sensed something was amiss. I deflected her questions as best I could, wolfed down my sandwich and soup and headed back to school.

I saw Carlo on the playground and asked him again if he knew where my pencil box had gone. Truthfully, he was one of my main suspects. He told me not to worry about the box, he knew who had taken it and he had stolen it back from the thief. However, now was not the time to talk about it. He would walk me home after school and give me the details. Carlo was so cool about the whole thing. Then he said, "Little *paisano*, I have your back. I think you are a smart kid and I don't want you to forget your friend Carlo when you move up. Somebody gives you trouble, you just call your buddy Carlo and I'll take care of it." We shook hands on it and I had a pleasant but anxious afternoon in the classroom. I was admonished by the teacher at recess that afternoon to take better care of my possessions. She shook down Carlo and the Jewish kid as they were her prime suspects. I left school that afternoon with Carlo, my *paisano* buddy, and headed for home.

We walked almost to my house when Carlo suddenly ducked into an alley and asked me to follow him. He reached inside his pants and pulled out my pencil box. He told me the following story. There was a kid in the Eagles that called Carlo a "flunkie" when we first entered the classroom that morning. At recess, he told Carlo that the two dumb "Dagos" (Italians) deserved to be the class stooges. Carlo said he noticed the kid asking the teacher at recess for permission to go back to the classroom early to go to the bathroom. After recess and during the chaos I caused about the missing pencil box, Carlo asked the teacher for permission to visit the bathroom. The bathroom was just a diversion; he checked the adjoining cloak room and found my pencil box hidden in the sleeve of the nasty kid's sweater.

Carlo believed the kid had seen the box on my desk during the morning session. Intent on stealing it he came back early from recess, took the box from my desk and put it in his sweater sleeve. Carlo took it from the kid's sweater and hid it in a storage box in the cloak room. He picked it up just before we departed for the day. I admired Carlo's sensitivity to all that was going on around him. I thanked him for helping me and all he said was, "Hey, we are *paisanos*." To be honest, I was never sure what *paisano* really meant but I knew it was working on my behalf. All was well at dinner that evening. While I filled in my parents and grandparents on my first day at school, I made no mention of the "Pencil Box Caper."

The next day before class began, Carlo took me aside and said, "That kid that stole your pencil box must be taught a lesson. I have worked it out with my friends. At recess today when I tell you to go to the monkey bars, get on them and go slowly forward. That's all you need to know." We had been on the playground for some time and were about to go in when Carlo said, "Go to the bars." I noticed the nasty kid was nearby and Carlo pushed him aside to let me get on the bars. The nasty kid said something about "Dagos" and got on the bars behind me. I went forward slowly with the nasty kid yelling at me to move faster. Suddenly, Carlo came running toward the monkey bars being chased by a second grader who was calling him names. Carlo turned his head to respond to the second grader. When he turned his head back, he saw that he was about to collide with the nasty kid hanging on the bars behind me. Carlo sidestepped and just brushed the nasty kid...but the second grader hit the kid squarely like a football tackle, pulling him from the bars and knocking him to the ground with a thump.

The nasty kid screamed in shock and pain; Carlo feigned a fall and was lying on the ground, moaning and holding his head. The second grader evaporated and could not be identified. The school nurse was called and in a few minutes an ambulance arrived. Carlo and the nasty kid were evacuated to a hospital. The nasty kid returned to school with multiple bruises and contusions. Carlo had a bump on his head. Carlo told me the next day the kid got what was coming to him and that we wouldn't be hearing him call us "Dagos" anymore. It didn't take a genius to understand that Carlo orchestrated the entire episode and the nasty kid was made to pay for his indiscretions; it was also noted that Carlo was the class enforcer and that I was his buddy.

I was in the first grade for two days and was the victim of a larceny and an accomplice in an assault. The only thing I was learning in school was self-defense. Unfortunately, I was also on the teacher's "usual suspects" list when anything went wrong in the classroom. It was time I took the initiative and went on the attack.

I quickly realized that the Lions were the teacher's darlings. They got more time with her on substantive learning those first few days. I listened closely to their instruction with the teacher when I should have been working on my Bee coloring book. The Busy Bees were tutored on matters of social obedience rather than letters and numbers. I was unsure of the full meaning of education but I knew that I wanted some; even more importantly, I knew I wasn't getting any while behavioral training was the Busy Bees lead subject. When the Busy Bees were next called to the front of the room for their time with the teacher, she began by teaching us the colors. Holding up a blue card, she asked who knew the name of that color. I did not wait for her to select someone to answer...it was time for action. I jumped up and in a slightly excited state, speaking rapidly, told her the color of the card she was holding was blue and the color of that other card was orange, another card was green and on and on until I covered all colors in the spectrum of light. I was like a child possessed and wouldn't shut up. I also told her I could read and began to read some words on the board that she had introduced to the Lions. I also told her I could add and subtract and demonstrated by going to the board and writing out a few simple addition problems and their answers. I recited the days of the week, the months of the year, counted to fifty and anything else I could think of.

When she finally got me to shut up by gently hugging me, my classmates were stunned at my behavior. I'm sure some thought I had a seizure as I was perspiring heavily. The teacher fortunately understood it all. She calmly wrote a word on the board and asked if I would read it for her. The word was "TOGETHER." At first I said, "To-get-her." The teacher told me to say all the syllables as one word. After a few tries I came up with the word "together" properly pronounced; but instead of just saying it, I shouted it out with joyous exclamation and pride. Led primarily by Carlo, the Busy Bees cheered at my success.

When the teacher restored order she went to her desk and took out a small box filled with gold stars. The stars would stick to a surface when wet with a liquid. She announced to the class that those students who excelled in her classroom would be rewarded with a gold star for their work. With that she ran one of those stars across her tongue and placed it in the center of my forehead. It was my first official decoration for a job well done. I received many more that year and my mother saved every one of them. The next day I was promoted to the Eagles. Then after six weeks, I was promoted to the Lions. Unsatisfied with being just a Lion, I wanted to be the best Lion. I was constantly and critically rating myself against the qualities of the other Lions in an effort to improve. As the year ended, I believed I was the second best Lion. The pretty girl with the long hair, who always dressed nicely, seemed to be the Number One Lion...academically and personally.

First grade was an altogether pleasant affair. I learned plenty and loved my teacher despite her continued efforts to muzzle my enthusiasm. Carlo and I remained sidekicks; I had the perfect situation...I was smart and I had reliable protection. Significantly, I was not remiss in sharing some of my knowledge with Carlo; albeit some of it was done illicitly. But...I had a debt to pay. In June we both matriculated to the second grade. Taking the initiative to demonstrate my knowledge base to the teacher was my premier moment in the first grade. I was no longer a stereotyped "Italian kid." I was Joey Laposata, a child who was serious about taking the initiative to get a proper education.

The "Take the Initiative" paradigm must always be focused on a positive outcome. The positive outcome I desired in the first grade was to get out of the Busy Bees and relocate to another group where I could meet my educational goals. I wanted some of that education the teacher was giving to the Lions and Eagles. That single episode in the first grade shaped my perspective of how to move ahead in life. I must confess that I had something inside of me that desired, or perhaps even compelled me, to seek out the more difficult tasks, the bigger projects and those unpleasant duties that others shunned. I loved to accomplish the tough jobs and solve difficult problems. The joy of doing the hard jobs successfully built my confidence to take the initiative. No fear, anxiety, stress or depression accompanied my taking the initiative to attain a goal. Taking the initiative solved problems or fixed a process that was broken. I loved the challenge of the task.

I also was smart enough to know that if it weren't broken, it did not require fixing. You must manage your initiative. If you get involved in too many ill-defined, improperly executed initiatives and talk about being "stressed out" you will likely be awarded the title of "Loose Cannon." That is an appellation difficult to lose.

As a young Army officer, one of my performance reports noted that I had a "single purposeness of mind" to be the best in everything I did. My rater then wrote that I was not well liked by my peers. People most likely to feel personally threatened by your initiative to do your best are those most likely to express their concern about your "single purposeness of mind." Simply, your elevated performance highlights their shortfalls. Make the choice to look after the men and women entrusted to your professional and personal care, stay on task and achieve your goals. Pay little attention to those who would fault you for your initiative to do your best. In my experience, integrity-based initiatives for the corporate good always trumped parochial, personal advancement goals.

One must also be prepared to back off from an initiative. When I first entered the Army there were many good men in my unit who had attended the US Military Academy at West Point. My regular army commission came via the Distinguished Military Graduate route at Indiana State College, located in Indiana, Pennsylvania. A week or two before the Army-Navy football game my Military Academy friends were at fever pitch about the game. I joined in the "Beat the Fish" chants at the bar in the club and really felt the spirit of the event. There was a planned gathering at the Officers' Club to watch the game on TV on Saturday. Since seats were limited, I signed up early. My best friend, whom I trusted and highly respected, was a Military Academy graduate. He came to me the day before the game and said, "Joe, there is some talk about your attendance at the game in the club. There are those who want to keep this event a closed affair; that is, just for Military Academy graduates. You are my friend and I do not want to see you hurt by these guys. Come if you like, and if something unpleasant occurs I will come to your aid. The decision is yours." Of course, I did not go to the game at the club. Taking a seat to watch the game produced no positive goal. Actually, it would only lead to negative outcomes blemishing the experience for the majority of West Point graduates who didn't care a bit about whether it was a closed or open event. I did not harbor any ill feelings nor did I feel any loss in not seeing the game. Retribution was not on my screen. I simply dropped my initiative to show support for the Army football team as an idea with no positive outcomes.

Initiative must be defined. Initiative must be managed. Initiative must be executed to produce positive outcomes. Make the higher choice to focus your initiatives to achieve positive, meaningful goals. The results of your effort will be enjoyed by many who follow you. They will reap the benefits of your initiative.

Make the choice to ensure your "Initiative revolver" is always loaded and prepared to fire. Just be certain your aim is directly at the target and that the target is an appropriate focus for your effort. Then, fire away with all your might.

CHAPTER SIX

BE A JOE DIMAGGIO

Inconspicuous Excellence

In both amateur and professional sport, athletes will frequently erupt into dances or other "Look at me" type behavior when they complete a play. While some find this entertaining, others find this self-inspired expression of the player's belief in the excellence of his performance to be a sham. Actually, it is usually nothing more than a brief show of self-promotion to hype a single achievement. Setting high standards and meeting them on a daily basis will produce a meaningful, lasting recognition of one's talent. Promote yourself by consistent high quality performance. The results are enduring and dancing is not required.

Early one summer evening in 1950 my father announced that we were leaving for Trenton, New Jersey immediately after dinner. Our trek from Johnstown, Pennsylvania to visit family in Trenton was an annual affair, but this trip was different. In addition to seeing relatives, my father also had arranged for a visit to Yankee Stadium to see Joe DiMaggio play. Having been baptized into the New York Yankee religion shortly after birth, I felt it was a dream come true to attend a game in Yankee Stadium, the house that Ruth built.

Dad's tactical surprise in announcing vacations at the last minute always sent us into a frenzy of packing and high anticipation of good things to come. Notably, my father never drove long distances during the day. We were nocturnal auto enthusiasts. The kids slept in pajamas in the back seat; up front, my mother and father drank coffee and talked softly all night long. We always arrived in Trenton just in time for breakfast.

On game day, my dad drove my brother Sammy and me to our Cousin Pete's home in Jersey City. We then took a train/subway to Yankee Stadium to watch the Yankees play the Detroit Tigers. Money being no object on such a momentous occasion, Dad sprung for front row seats along the third base line in the second deck. My brother Sammy had fallen into the Boston Red Sox heresy (his favorite player was Dominic DiMaggio), and he was something less than enthusiastic about the whole thing. He was doing only what was necessary to keep Dad off his back.

For me, merely entering the stadium was a thrill. The magnificence of Yankee Stadium convinced me that I was in a holy place – a holy place of baseball, at least. On the way to our seats, we passed a concession stand where I saw the most wonderful cup. It portrayed Joe DiMaggio in his home run swing on one side and the words "Be a Joe DiMaggio" on the other. I stopped my dad, knowing that I was not coming this way again soon, and said I wanted to buy the cup. Smooth as ever, he carefully examined the cup and asked me how much money I had on me. When I told him I had none, I saw my cousin go for his wallet but Dad waved him off; having lived with this man for twelve years, I knew that I would get the cup but there would be a price to pay.

Settling into our seats, my father laid out the ground rules for watching the game. We promised not only to watch the batter but also, with our peripheral vision, observe all the other players' positions and their movements when the ball was hit. He would be our guide in this matter; one did not come to this special place to loll in the sun, eat, and drink. Baseball was an art form; we were to absorb as much of it as possible under his tutelage.

The game began with a three-out inning for Detroit. In the bottom of the first inning, a Yankee batter hit a fly ball deep between the left and centerfielders. The Detroit centerfielder ran after the ball, but his legs pumped in an uncoordinated herky-jerky fashion, making a catch seem impossible. However, at the last moment, as the ball was about to strike the ground, he hurled himself in one great leap at the ball. With his arm fully outstretched, he caught the ball half-in and half-out of the webbing of the glove and dramatically slid across the outfield grass on his belly. When he stopped skidding, he jumped to his feet, held the ball triumphantly aloft, and pranced, holding the glove above his head with the ball half-trapped in the webbing, into the dugout. Yankee Stadium went wild with cheers and applause.

When I saw the catch, I got caught up in the action, leapt to my feet, and began to clap and yell like everyone else. My father sat quiet and motionless. He took my arm and said to me, "Sit down and be quiet. That was a lousy play. He should have caught that ball in his back pocket."

A few innings later, the Yankees were in the field. A Detroit batter hit the ball solidly into the deepest reaches of centerfield. By now my peripheral vision was in full operation. At the crack of the bat, I clearly saw Joe DiMaggio turn his back to home plate and run with long and graceful strides toward the wall, never looking back. At the precise moment he turned and the ball fell softly into his waiting glove. There was a titter of ho-hum applause in the stadium except for my father and me.

"Get on your feet," he screamed, "that was a great catch." We were yelling like maniacs, extolling the virtues of Joe's catch and advising everyone around us that the "Snow-shoe" playing centerfield for Detroit wouldn't have come within a country mile of making that play. Joe casually trotted back to the infield, dropped the ball near the pitcher's mound and headed for the dugout. He hesitated for a moment and then turned his head toward the third base second deck to see what that crazy man and his kid were cheering about. I saw his face; I waved to him and yelled, "Great catch, Joe!" To this day, I really think he smiled back.

Between innings my father said to me, "On occasion, people with mediocre talent, like the Detroit centerfielder, make a routine play look like something special. Because his catch seemed spectacular, he was instinctively praised for it. He then began to show off because he wanted to draw attention to himself, thinking it would gain him more visibility and respect for his talent. In truth, it was nothing of the sort. That guy will be in the minor leagues soon if he doesn't learn how to play centerfield."

"Joe DiMaggio just made a very difficult catch look easy. He didn't ask for applause by dancing around like the guy from Detroit. When he caught the ball, he knew that he made the difficult play look easy. Joe has done that so often the fans have come to expect the extraordinary from him. He plays baseball at a higher level and is admired and respected for meeting his elevated standards for playing the game. Dancing is not required." Then, tenderly, softly, he said the words that still give me goose bumps: "I know it will be difficult, but I want you to be a Joe DiMaggio."

As a boy, I had a tendency to show off. Dad frequently spoke to me about controlling that behavior. Unfortunately, I was making little progress and enjoyed performing. No doubt about it, I knew exactly what he was talking about. Being in Yankee Stadium with Joe DiMaggio on the field, it was like an oath when I said to him, "Dad, I will really try." He smiled, and we went on with the game. We had lots of hot dogs, peanuts, and soft drinks that day. On the way out, he bought me the cup *and* an official New York Yankee miniature bat. I left the stadium a happy kid, a little smarter, and even more devoted to my father than before.

Taking that oath in Yankee Stadium to continue to do my very best but not show off in the process made a difference in my life. Results were not exactly immediate, but Dad knew when, where, and how to cut a deal.

My father knew that to be respected, one must earn the respect of others. The way to earn that respect is to develop a high standard of excellence in your life, one that sets you apart from others. Then, that high standard must be repeatedly demonstrated until exceptional performance is considered routine. A quiet, efficient performance is the quickest way to gain respect and recognition. He made certain I understood that when you are respected for your work, personal satisfaction is not derived from dancing to the dugout but from an inner sense of knowing that that you did your very best in meeting your own high standards.

Dad said, "Showing off doesn't give you a feeling of satisfaction…it is just the opposite. Because you know in your heart that you are not what you made yourself out to be, you will always feel some anxiety that you will be found out. Showing off is a form of a lie. It won't be pleasant when you are exposed."

Visiting Mount Vernon, the home of George Washington, Dad saw an inscription describing the life of one of General Washington's relatives. It said the man possessed the quality of "inconspicuous excellence" in his life. My father loved that phrase. He used it to describe men and women who set high personal and professional standards and lived their lives accordingly. To his dying day, he worked to instill the spirit of inconspicuous excellence into my life. Among his last words of counsel to me was that I was to beware of the flashy performer. He said, "Flashy people are usually potential-poor. If they are working for you, their shortcomings will be an albatross around your neck." He made it clear that it was the long-term, high quality performers who had the "right stuff" to do the hard jobs, even in the most difficult of times.

I made the choice to follow his advice and suppressed the show-off gene, living my life by my father's code of inconspicuous excellence. I also chose to surround myself with men and women of inconspicuous excellence. This was one of the best choices I ever made. I promise there is absolutely nothing inconspicuous about inconspicuous excellence. It shines like a bright light in the darkness.

CHAPTER SEVEN

HEY BOY, LIGHT MY CIGAR

Avoid Acts of Retribution

It is not uncommon to experience being offended in word or deed by another person. It is also quite common for the aggrieved person to seek some form of retribution for the perceived offense. The movie "The Godfather" is a monument to retribution and the concept of success being measured by those "who lost the least." Satisfaction derived from "getting even" is short lived. The old adage, "What you do not want done to yourself, do not do unto others," remains an appropriate rule for managing the issue of retribution. If you choose the path of retribution, you have chosen disharmony in your life.

My grandfather played the mandolin and was keen on my developing musical skills at an early age. According to my mother, my grandparents gave me a xylophone as a present when I was five years old to foster an interest in music.

The xylophone had a large "1" in the middle of a wooden bar. Directly below the "1" was the letter "C." On each succeeding bar, that process was repeated with the notes of the chromatic scale and a corresponding number. The music book that accompanied the xylophone permitted a child to play songs by identifying the scale note as well as the number. Because I knew my numbers at age five, I learned how to use this instrument and soon played songs from the music book. I was so taken by my talent that I banged on the xylophone at every opportunity and began to commit songs to memory by remembering a sequence of numbers rather than notes. My parents were convinced that they had a budding Mozart on their hands. Accordingly they bought me a very small accordion and took me to a teacher for private lessons. The teacher was a very kind and patient woman. She did not permit me to do the numbers routine and schooled me in reading music. In short order, I managed to play the instrument with as much skill as a five-year-old kid could muster.

A year later my father learned of auditions for a minstrel show that traveled to school auditoriums in the local area during the winter. They agreed that it would be a good idea to give me some experience on stage and my parents took me for a tryout. There were three acts open for children. Dressed in my "darling little Italian boy" velvet suit with short pants, knee socks and loafers and with a smile pasted on my face, I played my songs for three gentlemen. They accepted me to perform in a few weekend shows. I had a delightful time on stage, never had stage fright, and found the show business routine to be an enhancement to my young ego. All went well until the last show of the season.

I always performed third behind two teen-aged brothers with a magic act and a baton-twirling girl who was older than I. Both acts were very good and always received lots of applause. We were all quite pleasant with one another. During that last show, when the baton-twirling girl left the stage, she paused before passing me. Smiling and putting her face close to mine, in the singsong voice that little girls often use to antagonize little boys, she said softly, sweetly, and directly to me, "And now ladies and gentlemen, the squirt with the squeeze box." I knew that she was making fun of me as I was introduced as "Little Joey Laposata, the Accordion Virtuoso." Laughing, she quickly disappeared but she had pushed a button that I didn't know that I had. The first two acts had the audience pumped up and the girl's comment got me all fired up. I entered the stage smiling and waving to a nice round of applause (and a lot of OOOHHHs from the older ladies).

My first song was a polka that I played as if I were Frankie Yankovic, "The Polka King." A roar of applause followed. Then I played "Home Sweet Home," and on the second verse, I played *and* sang the song. This was a variation on the scripted performance but the girl had me fired up. On one knee, I finished the song, a la Al Jolson, and crooned out, "And there's noooo place like hooooome." The audience went wild. I ran off the stage smiling, waving, and throwing kisses. I was brought back for a curtain call. I looked for the little girl to give her a smirk from the "squirt" but she was gone.

On the way home my father asked, "Why did you change your routine?" I told him the "squirt" story and thus began an uncountable number of counseling sessions on the malevolent nature of "getting even." My family did not look upon *vendetta*, the Sicilian version of retribution, kindly. I tried to overcome this urge. But if aggrieved, I needed satisfaction and enjoyed making the other guy squirm.

In grade school, during a recess, the class bully pushed me to the ground calling me a "Dago" in the process. In response, when the cold weather arrived, on three occasions over a period of four months, I surreptitiously lifted the bully's left glove or mitten from his coat pocket and stuffed it in a storage box in the cloakroom marked "Easter Supplies." The bully was from a poor family so when he came up missing his hand wear, he would tell one and all how his mother "beat his butt" for losing his gloves. By spring, he was wearing one glove and one mitten, both right handed, to school. My pleasure in the matter abounded, and I feigned joyful surprise when the teacher opened the box at Easter and found the gloves. It was then that I knew that I had been infected with the "vendetta" gene. I truly enjoyed it.

After repeated attempts by my parents and grandparents to suppress this tendency, it all came to a head one evening in my father's barbershop when I was fifteen years old. We had a customer who was a mean and nasty man but a very faithful patron. He would never arrive while the shop was open but would come to the back door wanting his hair cut when the blinds were down and the doors locked. He often asked me to brush his coat, carry something to his car, or do some other menial task. I didn't like the guy.

I was filling an Iron City beer can cigarette lighter with lighter fluid when the nasty guy arrived at the back door one evening. To fill the lighter, one removed the cap and squeezed a container of lighter fluid into the tightly packed cotton in the body of the can. It was imperative to let this sit for a few minutes, then strike the flint wearing a glove. There was always an excess of lighter fuel when the flint was first struck, and it was like watching the Hindenburg airship explode. A loud "poooouf" accompanied by a blue flame and black smoke left a soot residue covering everything nearby.

When the nasty man got into the barber chair, he turned to me and said, "Hey, boy, light my cigar." I didn't like his tone of voice but I grabbed the lighter and went to the chair. The cigar had been lit before and was now half its original size. He had it clenched in his teeth, his evil face contorted, eyes half-closed, and his lips not touching the cigar. I hesitated for an instant, knowing that I had just filled the lighter and the probable outcome when I lit the cigar. I also knew the outcome would be something less than acceptable to my father. The man growled, "Come on, boy, light the damned cigar." That was all I needed. My "vendetta" was at hand.

I took the Iron City beer can lighter, placed it under the cigar tip, which was just beyond the end of his nose, and struck the flint. In an instant there was a loud "Whump" sound and a flash of light. The cold blue flame engulfed my hand and Mr. Nasty's nose. There was the commingled smell of lighter fluid and burning hair. After the fireworks, I noticed that my hand was black with soot. Mr. Nasty's face was another thing. The flame left a near perfect outline, in black soot, of its explosive path, completely covering the man's nose, artistically curving and narrowing while passing between his eyebrows and coming to a point directly in the middle of his forehead. His eyebrows were singed and smoldering slightly, while a thin wisp of tobacco smoke rose from the end of the cigar.

In a nanosecond my father understood what had happened and went into damage control mode. Fortunately, no one was injured. I was dismissed and, though I was to see the man many times afterwards, neither of us ever spoke of the incident. Only once, months later, when Mr. Nasty was brushing off his own coat, he did say, "Joe, that kid of yours is dangerous." The case was closed. I had my vendetta although I would forever claim it was the lighter's fault. I had my story and I was sticking to it.

Shortly thereafter on a Monday, my father said to me, "Joe, I want you to help me replace the magazine stand in the shop." The shop was closed on Monday, the only school day of the week that I could play basketball at the playground. I worked or attended church activities after school Tuesday through Friday and all day on Saturday. I reported my scheduling conflict to my father without malice. He said, "I want to be certain that I understand. You will not help me today because you are going to the playground." I assured him that that was the case; even though a voice in the back of my head suggested that I would live to regret the move.

The acquisition of a driver's learning permit was a teenage milestone of great importance to me. I had a graphic posted on the wall in the pantry indicating the number of days remaining until that glorious event. For almost a year I had kept everyone advised of the days remaining until that wonderful moment arrived. My ever-supportive mother talked my father into having the Notary come to our house for the signing of the paperwork requesting the permit.

She arranged for a celebration with food and drinks, inviting everyone in our family circle to share in my joy on that important day. On the appropriate day, at the appropriate hour, the Notary arrived at our home. He was a cheerful Irish fellow, liked by all. Our kitchen was good-sized and was filled shoulder to shoulder with the people I loved most. All went quiet as the Notary began to ask me questions as he filled out the form. I smiled broadly while giving him the answers. As he finished the form, he said to my father, "Now, Joe, please tell me what you want me to do about the date of the request for learner's permit."

My father took center stage and delivered his now famous soliloquy on retribution. Turning to me he said, "A few months ago I asked you to help me repair the magazine rack in the shop. You advised me that it was more important for you to play basketball with your friends than to work with me. There is a commandment passed to Moses, many years ago, which compels children to honor their father and their mother. It says nothing about honoring your friends. You failed to honor me.

"You have a character defect concerning your need for 'vendetta' when you feel dishonored. We have not been able to suppress that trait. It is time for you to understand my seriousness about mending this defect. You have violated my honor and now I demand my 'vendetta.'"

He turned to the Notary and said, "Pat, date the application for one month from now. Joe, you will wait and I will have my 'vendetta.'"

This Sicilian turn of events was more than the jovial Gallic Notary could stand. The poor guy sat open-mouthed and stunned. He should have been the official that initiated great joy in our home. Now he was the matador goring the young bull. My Aunt Sara, who defended me even when I was wrong, rose in my defense. My grandfather advised her to be quiet as this was my father's affair. A very close friend of my father, Joe Taranto, said, "Is there any way we can work something out here? He is a good boy; we all make mistakes." My dad remained silent behind his hard Sicilian face. It was checkmate; I was cooked. I was going to have to wait another thirty days to get the learner's permit.

My grandmother had an intuition for this sort of thing. Many events in the Sicilian household have endings like a Jack London novel. God bless her, she stood and said in a firm voice, "Time will cure all of this. There is no damage done but it is an important lesson to be learned. Let's have something to eat and a glass of wine. We will all feel better." She offered kind wisdom for both sides and something for the stomach; it was accepted by all. My grandfather stepped forward and ensured my Dad and I shook hands and embraced warmly. We all had a good laugh over "Joey, the hard head" learning another lesson.

My brother, Sammy "Clean Hands," was in shock. We were long time roommates and I think this hurt him a little. He knew of my intense feelings about getting the learner's permit and he was a sensitive kid. My sister, Dolly, cut from the same piece of cloth as I, smelled an opportunity to tease and was having a good time. Brother Michael was a baby and was laughing only because everyone else was laughing.

My mother hugged and kissed me, saying, "Your father is right about the vendetta business, you know. He thought you were skillful in taking your vendetta on Mr. Nasty, but he will not tolerate that kind of behavior. You must change your ways." Dear Aunt Sara, hugging and kissing me, said she loved me no matter what diabolical punishment my father devised. There were no tantrums and no hard feelings on my part. I was disappointed to be sure, but it was only a flesh wound. My father had a right to keep me on the straight path, and he had skillfully done it one more time.

Before I went to bed that evening, he said, "Joe, I hope you understand the negative effects of vendetta. You must let it go. If I exacted my vendetta each time someone was rude to me, I would have a full time job. Don't take men like the nasty guy personally; understand they have a problem lurking somewhere in their lives that incites this kind of behavior. Just smile, be nice and move on." I went to my room vowing to keep that trait under control. It has taken much self-discipline and prayer to live up to that vow.

At Christmas my father gave me a set of keys to the car and a house key. "You can use the car anytime you want," he said. "Tell me when you are going to take it and where you are going. Never do anything on the road that will endanger yourself or others." I drove my father's car almost daily and always told him when I was taking it and where I was going. I never did anything to endanger myself or anyone else. He was the Alpha Male in the house and I knew it. The retribution issue was closed.

My father's strict guidance was that there is no place in the human experience for acts of retribution. There is nothing positive about it, and the outcomes are, by their very nature, intended to be hurtful. One must diligently strive to never willfully retaliate for some perceived slight. Retribution has a way of magnifying and sustaining itself. Those who are successful in achieving retribution are themselves frequently victims, at a later date, of some form of retaliation.

It takes persistent self-discipline, courage and the putting aside of pride to work out differences. If issues seemingly cannot be resolved, expose the situation and seek professional assistance. A declaration of retributive family or corporate warfare is not an option. There will be no winners. The bloody scenes of retribution in the movie *The Godfather* clearly illustrate the "no win" aspect of vendetta warfare where success is measured by those "who lost the least."

Having lived through a culture of retribution in an organization, I assure you it impedes organizational growth, fosters poor performance, and exacts a toll of extraordinary anxiety and stress on those working in that environment. In the corporate world, I have seen retribution, or the fear of retribution, send more than one person to the grave. The diligent and caring are the first to go. Mental pain and stress are killers. The persistence of this malady is phenomenal. Never be an enabler of retribution even when it is what everyone else is doing. It takes a strong change manager to wipe out this plague in an organization.

A response to an act of retribution must be direct, unemotional, and focused; confrontation with the intent to resolve the issue is one thing, retribution is another. Candid discussion of grievances, with controlled emotions, will go a long way towards creating a happier life. It is not easy, but you will be respected for your desire to be above retaliation.

The bottom line of retribution management is to take aggressive action to resolve issues but avoid initiating acts of retribution. In short, work it out. If you choose the path of retribution, the outcomes are guaranteed to be painful and unpleasant to your life and career when you are found out. Retribution is a bad choice.

CHAPTER EIGHT

"GIMME A NICKEL OR
I WILL BREAK YOUR WINDOW

Random Acts of Kindness

*With so many individuals and organizations asking for dona-
tions, our sense of charity has become dulled. In truth, opportunities for responsible charity abound. It only requires common
sense to complement the character trait of charity to assist those
who are truly in need. Remain sensitive to others and be responsible in your charity. It is our duty to our fellow man.*

After Chandler Elementary School released students for
summer holiday, I began working five days a week in my father's barber shop as cashier, shoeshine boy and janitor. One
day in early June at lunchtime, a young boy about eight or
nine years old burst into the shop with a rock in his hand. In
a loud and aggressive voice he said to my father, "Gimme a
nickel or I will break your window." This boy was well

known. He was from a nearby poor family; he was also small and was bullied by many of the other kids. His response to his situation was aggression; he was angry at the world. On this particular day he was filthy dirty. I clearly remember that one of his tattered canvas shoes was torn, secured to his foot by a heavy duty rubber strap that passed beneath the sole of the shoe and over the top of his foot.

One husky steel worker waiting for a haircut was prepared to propel the kid back into the street but my father stepped forward, got down on one knee and looked the kid directly in the eye. He said in very even tones, "If I give you the nickel, what are you going to do with it?" The kid, still belligerent, replied, "I'm going to your store next door and buy some candy." My father responded in a kind voice, "Did you have breakfast this morning?" The boy sharply replied, "No." My dad asked him if he was hungry. The kid hesitantly and almost ashamedly said that he was.

My dad turned to me and said, "Get your mother." My mother stopped what she was doing in the kitchen and quickly went to the shop. My father said, "Mary, this young man has not had breakfast. Please see that he has a proper lunch." After looking the kid over, my mother told my dad quite clearly that the kid was not coming into her clean home. Dad calmly said, "Feed him on the back porch." Then he said something to her in Italian, and she turned to me and said, "Joey, come with me."

Mom took me to our outside water spigot in back of the building, gave me a towel, soap and shampoo and directed, "Strip him to his underwear and have him put his clothes in this shopping bag." Turns out he was not wearing underwear, so the scrubbing began "au natural." My mother rejected the first cleaning; so I told the kid, "Let's do this right so we can get some lunch." That seemed to motivate him. When he finished, Mom said, almost as an afterthought, "Rinse him off with the hose." He stood there smiling while

I turned the hose nozzle on "STRONG" and washed off any soap residue. Then she came out with an old tooth brush and tooth powder. She made the kid brush his teeth. Finishing up he was buck naked, freshly hosed down, and had a clean mouth. Apparently, he was finally prepared to my mother's standard for dining.

Mom had a full set of clean clothes, including underwear, laid out for the kid on the porch. After he dried off she had him get dressed under her supervision. While the clothes were those we had outgrown or were a bit worn, they sort of fit the kid. My mother was cut from first sergeant cloth and she was in full charge of our home. When she told the kid to sit on the swing, comb his hair and be quiet, he obeyed. He and I spoke about the cleaning episode. He told me it felt nice to smell good.

In short order my mother appeared with a large bologna sandwich on her homemade bread with lettuce and tomato, potato chips and a large glass of milk. My mom told him to eat slowly and watched him eat everything. She asked if he wanted more and the kid said, "Can you make me one more of everything?" After the kid had eaten a full second helping, Mom gave him an apple. She then appeared with a pair of shoes that were delivered by the son of the preacher at the Brethren Church.

Properly fed, re-clothed, and scrubbed down to his dermis, my mother said to me, "Take the boy back to your father." I had advised the kid to thank my mother for the food and clothes. To my surprise, he responded on cue with a smile and a "Thank you." He left our porch with his old clothes in a paper bag. When my dad saw him, he asked if he had been fed, made some nice comment about his personal sanitation and the serviceable clean clothes. He then asked the boy in front of everyone in the shop, "Do you still need a nickel?" The kid actually teared up and said, "No, Mr. Laposata. I told Mrs. Laposata thanks for everything."

With that, my father went to the cash register, took out a nickel and gave it to the kid. The boy was overcome and really started bawling. One customer got up and comforted the kid. After order was restored, the kid left and everyone felt good about my parents' actions.

My father had me get my mother and thanked her in front of all the customers. One wise guy customer asked, "If I came in for a haircut, dirty and nasty, asking for a nickel would my father take pity on him and have my mother feed him a plate of her pasta?" That was the comic relief that ended the episode, but I was extremely proud of my parents' responsible act of charity.

That evening I spoke with my father about the incident. I told him that my inclination had been to kick the kid out into the street and call the cops. He told me the key to reacting to this kind of situation was to keep a clear mind and quickly assess the situation. One must never lose control of the situation by responding to one's emotions. Having lived through the Great Depression, he had seen many hungry people. He told me that experience helped him quickly understand the kid's situation. Getting my mother into the act was his way of feeding and cleaning up the kid while demonstrating how our family operated. He said my cheerful following of his direction was helpful in setting an example for the kid to emulate. My dad made it a point that the boy was to retain whatever dignity he had and to treat him with courtesy was essential.

My father also made certain I was alerted to perform acts of kindness as a teenager. I accompanied him in delivering food to sick neighbors, going to the hospital to give a haircut to a sick customer (he never charged for a hospital haircut), and visiting families who had just had a death to be certain their immediate welfare was in place. "Acts of kindness are good for the mind and the soul," he explained. "They just make you feel good and make the recipient of your thoughtfulness feel even better. You will always sleep deeper when you responsibly help others who require your talent and resources."

He made sure I understood these deeds were to be low key events...no publicity, no fanfare, just a simple demonstration of one man's affection and response to someone in genuine need. Little did I know then that the human intellect absorbs situations like this one osmotically and stores them away for replication at some later date. Being around my father every day and watching him manage simple acts of charity expanded my capability to respond instinctively to similar issues that arose in my life.

In my first year in the Army I decided to apply my father's "Christmas Visit" approach to those under my command. I had only one married junior soldier who was living off the post. I decided to visit him and his wife with a small basket of fruit. He was perhaps 18 or 19 years old and his wife was 16 and... they had a baby. I had trouble finding his home because he was living in a garage in an alley. The place was heated by a plug-in electric heater. They had to go outside to use the bathroom. I was struck by the poverty in which they were living. I immediately advised my platoon sergeant of the situation. He took over and raised a few dollars to help them through Christmas. He had some NCO wives oversee the welfare of the poor young girl and her baby. The sergeant did a super job in straightening out that situation. The young soldier and his family had a better holiday because of the NCO's act of charity. I thanked my father's example of sensitizing me to respond to the welfare of others. Acts of charity are not planned; they just seem to occur as a response to a genuine human need. It is our responsibility to note a need and act positively to assist.

In my lifetime I have tried to follow my father's lead on the matter of charity. I will never be as successful at doing nice things for people when they least expect it as Dad was. It was second nature to him; I have to work at being thoughtful. I recently had the opportunity to assist a woman attain recognition for her work in helping others. It was an act of affection for a kind and caring person. After the award ceremony, one of her friends came to me and thanked me profusely for what I had done. She said, "Your random act of kindness meant more to her than you will ever know. Thank you for being so kind to our friend." With those words, my father's counsel came back to me in a flash.

I try not to think much about these acts of charity, but when I'm having some difficulty going to sleep, I remember some long ago story about doing something good for someone. I am fast asleep in short order. Choose to perform responsible random acts of kindness and your reward in return will be exponential to your effort...and your sleep will be contented, deep and restful.

One word of caution: Acts of charity must be associated to verifiable need. Giving money to panhandlers on the street does not fall into that category. In New York City I was once confronted by a man outside a pub asking for money. I said, "No" and walked away. I felt bad that I had not helped him. Walking a little farther down the street, I felt extraordinary guilt, so I turned around to return and give him some coins. Approaching, I observed the man receive money from a passerby. He thanked the woman, blessed her and then turned around and walked back into the bar. The poor woman had hoped to bring some goodness into the panhandler's life but in fact she was really an enabler of the man's self-indiscipline. My guilt in this matter was relieved.

Make the choice to be sensitive to the needs of others and be responsible in your charity and do it without fanfare for an added good feeling. That done, be responsible in your charity so that it produces positive outcomes rather than subsidizing the continuance of irresponsible behavior. One of the greatest character traits is responsible charity. Being a charitable person is a choice you must practice.

CHAPTER NINE

THE DOG POO PIE PAN PRANK

An Insight into Contrition and Forgiveness

"How to forgive is something we have to learn, not as a duty or obligation but as an experience akin to the experience of love; it must come into being spontaneously."

T. C. Speers

Our home in Kernville was a traditional structure on a quiet, tree-lined street with few children. When we moved to Oakhurst in the west end of Johnstown, there were far more children my age than there had been in Kernville. However, the house in Oakhurst was behind and above our store and shops; it was noisy, next to a beer garden and adjacent to a trolley transfer point that was a hubbub of activity at shift changes in the steel mills and coal mines. In my estimation, the house was a catastrophe, but I had a great time with the new kids. After a fashion, they began to share closely guarded neighborhood secrets.

I learned how to get an apple out of a grouchy neighbor's tree without getting caught, how to perfectly flatten a penny on the trolley's street rails and on Halloween a veritable cornucopia of tricks were revealed. It was on my first Halloween in Oakhurst that I was invited to observe an ingenious, hilarious and thrilling Halloween "trick."

The word on the street was that a group of teenagers were going to pull off a big time Halloween prank near our neighborhood. We didn't know *what* was going down but did know *who* was going to do the job. When the older guys began to drift away from the submarine sandwich shop that Halloween evening we knew the countdown had begun. We younger guys followed at a distance. When we saw them assemble near the target house, we hid out in the alley overlooking the scene. The teenagers had collected a sizeable amount of fresh dog dung in a heavy paper bag. We watched as they sprinkled lighter fluid on the bag and, with a large pie pan in hand, infiltrated an old man's property.

The following was executed with the precision of a military operation. One kid, almost crawling on his belly, went onto the porch and placed the pie pan down directly in front of the door. The bag of dog dung was swiftly placed on the pie pan and lit. It erupted into flames. Another boy ran to the porch and began ringing the doorbell, pounding on the door, and yelling loudly. The teenagers then exited quickly into the night. When the old man opened the door, he saw the burning bag and began yelling, "Fire, Fire!"

He then stomped on the bag to extinguish the flames. It was only when he had put the fire out that he realized that he had been sabotaged. With one shoe freshly coated in dog dung, he ran into the street vowing the things he would do to those who had played that Halloween prank. To say the least, I was impressed. Those teenaged commandos had done a super job. For some unexplainable reason, I was excited by the smooth execution of the plan and wanted to give it a try. Back at the sub shop the teenagers were heroes. Someone even bought them a sandwich with extra meat!

Since most young boys consider all forms of vertebrate bodily waste highly amusing, I wanted in on the fun. As I saw it, no harm was done (if you did not count one soiled, stinky shoe). I was sure I could do it. I gathered two younger kids as my disciples during the following year and revealed my plan for the Stinky Shoe Trick on the next Halloween. Like every good military operation this event had to have a code name. Mustering all my verbal skills, I came up with "Dog Poo Pie Pan." Say it fast and it's even funnier because it sounds like something on a menu at an Oriental restaurant. Every time we thought about the trick we would convulse in laughter.

We had a perfect victim. He was a cranky old man who lived alone in a small house. His place was a few blocks from my home with an escape route through the alleyways. Since most of the alleys were dark, I figured we would not be recognized even if someone did see us. We rehearsed the plan like it was D-Day. Halloween arrived and we were ready. We wore dark sweatshirts and black knit hats. When it was sufficiently dark, we went into action. One of my partners in crime was a veritable dog poo magnet. Where he got it all I don't know but it represented the work of many dogs and, by the looks of it, some quite large. I was the pie pan and dog poo bag guy; Eddie was the door banger and screamer. We pulled the trick off with precision. The old man got his shoe filled with Nature's Best, and boy was he angry! We vanished into the night stopping only when we were near my home. Off came the caps and sweatshirts as we headed to Clark's Dairy store at the corner for a soda. Oh, the joy of a job well done; the Coca-Cola never tasted sweeter.

The next day at dinner, my father nonchalantly asked me, "What did you do last evening?" I told him honestly that I was in the neighborhood "tricking and treating." He asked if I was in the vicinity of the street where the old man lived. Instantly, I knew he was on to something. I couldn't lie to my father but wasn't offering any information either. He continued with his line of direct questioning better than anything you will see on a TV lawyer show. I broke under the prosecutor's examination. When my father added that he had an eyewitness and described our getaway in detail, I knew I was cooked. I failed to remember that almost everyone knew my dad. Also I failed to appreciate that in our close-knit neighborhood everyone knew to whom I belonged. A customer saw me from his back porch as I passed beneath the lone streetlight, fleeing the scene in my commando costume. The noise created by the man after our Dog Poo Pie Pan caper had alerted the "stoolie" to the event and, having seen me run in the opposite direction, he put two and two together. Dutifully, he reported the details to my dad.

My father had a repertoire of prepared lectures that he used when my behavior was, in his estimation, "only one step above the animals." This time he was so fired up that I got them all like a blast from a machine gun. Only my familiarity with his lectures permitted me to follow the general trend of his tirade. My mother was horrified; how could I have done such a thing to a poor old man? My brother and sister were alight with glee at seeing me being roasted again. It all came to a head when my father asked me, "What do you have to say for yourself?" In my most heartbroken voice I said, "Dad, I'm sorry." He banged both hands on the table as he stood up and in a loud voice repeated, "You're sorry? I don't want *words* of contrition, I want *acts* of contrition. Get your coat."

My dear old dad never struck me but I often would have preferred some form of corporal punishment as opposed to the devious, protracted, ingenious punishments he devised. My protective mother advised my father not to do anything rash. I might have been a bad puppy but was still her puppy and nobody messed with her puppies. The big dog wasn't talking; he was a man with a mission. Without speaking a word we marched to the old man's house.

When the old man came to the door he recognized my father and invited us in. When I saw how badly he was living compared to us, my contrition became real. I had never seen anyone live like that. He had an upright open flame gas heater in the living room. The room was swarming with a cacophony of odors because he had been heating food over the vent on the top and some of the food had boiled over. The old man had not cleaned off the residue; it just turned to ash and burned off the heater. He was wearing an old, dirty shirt and even dirtier trousers. He needed a haircut and a shave. His house slippers had seen better days and his personal hygiene was suspect. I was in culture shock.

My father spoke in a gentle but embarrassed tone explaining, in graphic detail, what I had done. He was making a confession for me to the old man, and he did a pretty good job of it. The old man was impressed with my father's sense of morality (understanding right from wrong), and when my father finished, the old man turned to me and said, "Son, what do you have to say for yourself?"

Now I may have done something dumb the night before, but I was not stupid. Picking up on my father's last statement at our house I said, "Sir, I am sorry. I know those are just words, so please allow me to make it up to you in some way."

The old gentleman could tell I was sincere, and so he said, "Since my wife died, I haven't been able to keep up with things around here and I could use a little help. Could you see your way clear to come by from time to time to help me a bit?" Since my father was not one for ill-defined tasks, he said, "Let's make this a contract: Joey will be here to help you every day after school for a week. After a week, we will look at things, and you and I will decide how much more work he has to do." This pleased the old man.

For the next few days my relationship with my father could best be described as "icy." When he did speak to me, what he had to say came out in the form of a growl. My mother's affection sustained me along with the sure knowledge that Dad couldn't stay angry forever, it just seemed that way.

The first day at the old man's house was hell. Trash was everywhere - in the kitchen, living room, bathroom, and bedroom. Also, on the back porch was that one smelly shoe. Cleaning it was among my first tasks in the order of business. I did my best to clean the house, but the junk was in layers and little progress was made. I had to ask the old man what he wanted done with each item I uncovered. Since he was a chatty old guy, little headway was made. When I asked for a garbage can, he produced one already full of junk. I had to go to a local store a few streets away to get some empty boxes for the rest of it.

After a few days, I managed to get the living room and the kitchen reasonably well cleaned. I then went to my sainted mother for help in getting the place ready for my father's inspection. She came with me the next day and pitched in. She had plenty of orders and instructions for me, and under her good guidance, real progress ensued.

The old man liked my mother and talked to her constantly. For the first time I realized just how lonely he was. She told him I was a good boy and that I had never done anything like this before. The old man said that he was grateful for my parents' course of action and that he hoped to have me around for some time. When my mother finished (she even gave me a spray that made the place smell better), the house was now prepared for my father's critical eye.

My father inspected the house and was impressed with the outcome. The old man and I had sort of become friends that week. He called me "Joey" and I called him "Sir." Notably, the old man shaved and put on a clean but worn shirt for my father's visit. The old man asked if I could continue to help out once or twice a week for a while. My father agreed. The next week when I went to his house, I delivered an Italian dinner my mother had prepared for him.

The old man wanted to eat it right away while it was still hot. I asked him what he wanted me to do while he ate. He said, "Just sit with me and let's talk." Over my mother's lasagna and salad, he told me of his two children who didn't visit very often. He told me how lonesome he was, now that his wife had died. He admitted that sometimes he was not in a good disposition towards others because he was so alone. The old man said he really didn't mean it when he yelled at us kids, but sometimes anger just came out when he was really lonely. I began to share news about school with him; he always laughed at my stories. From that day forward we were friends.

Shortly thereafter the old man told my father that I had completed my Act of Contrition and that he was sure that I had learned my lesson. I was relieved of any responsibility for further contractual visits to the old man, but I couldn't stay away. I was drawn to him by something that I didn't understand, at least not back then. When he was our target, he was a faceless, grouchy old man. Now that I had come to know him as a person, I had a genuine affection for the old guy.

I would sometimes stop in for a few minutes on my way home from school to talk to my friend and help him out in some way. Sometimes I'd deliver something my mother had prepared for him to eat. I always sat with him to chat while he dined, noticing that he was beginning to keep himself, his house and his porch clean all on his own. One day the old man told me that his son was going to have him move in with his family on a farm in the next county. He didn't know when he would go but that it would be soon. I came back a few days later, and he was still there and we talked a bit. But the next time I visited, he was gone.

He left an envelope tucked in the door jam with my name on it. The content of the letter inside was touching, even to a young boy. He wanted me to know that he was never really mad at me for what I did and that this letter was his Act of Forgiveness. He also wrote that he enjoyed my company and that I had brightened up his life. He noted that my father was a brave man to bring his son to another man to confess a wrongdoing and then have the kid do penance to boot. He wanted me to tell my mother that she was a wonderful cook and that he delighted in her Italian dinners and her Christmas cookies. He left me with these words: "You will do well in life. Your parents will not allow you to do less." The old man disappeared from my life, but he has remained in my heart. Funny, I still like to say "dog poo pie pan;" I just don't play that game anymore.

My behavior that Halloween night falls into the "What Were You Thinking?" category. My father's rejection of shallow *words* of contrition and insistence on *acts* of contrition has been burned into my brain. It has served me well in my adult life. Many errant soldiers have performed acts of contrition to account for their "What Were You Thinking?" behavior. Everyone makes mistakes. The important thing is to learn from them and never repeat your errant behavior. When harm results from your errors in judgment, you must do something to make amends. My Dog Poo Pie Pan prank was certainly something less than brilliant and actually quite dangerous. Out of that experience I learned two valuable lessons. First, contrition and forgiveness are entwined. Demonstrated contrite repentance is the critical path in resolving day-to-day anomalies in human behavior. In short, if you screwed it up, fix it promptly and sincerely. The icing on the cake comes when the aggressor and the aggrieved make their peace and genuine forgiveness is acknowledged.

Secondly, I learned that goodness exists in people even when not readily visible. The old man was not a grouch; he was a lonely man who occasionally became grouchy. With just a small charitable effort, mutual respect and friendship are predictable outcomes. Some small sign of affection like a dish of pasta, a clean living room, and a little genuine friendship will incite positive feelings in a person's heart. Deal with people for who they are. It will require an investment of your spirit and it often requires a special persistence to do it properly. You will get burned on occasion with this technique, but when it works, the joy of success is so sweet that the pain of failure is forgotten.

The wisdom of the actions and the words of forgiveness and friendship from a lonely old man live with me today. When you find an equivalent of the old man, treat him or her with friendship, respect, and dignity. That person will certainly find reward in your charitable kindness. The voice you hear in your head when all is quiet at night will tell you that you have served well and that some force greater than you is pleased with your stewardship. That is true emotional tranquility.

Be sensitive to issues of contrition and forgiveness. They are the perfect choices to consider when dealing with errant human behavior.

CHAPTER TEN

IF IT LOOKS LIKE APPLESAUCE...

Choose Good Friends Wisely

Words of wisdom concerning friends are plentiful. "You are known by the company you keep," "A true friend will never let you down," and, "Make no man your friend before inquiring how he has used his former friends," are catch phrases learned early in life. Be advised that choosing a friend is as important as choosing a competent, talented doctor. Bad friends and bad doctors will hasten your demise.

I have always considered myself fortunate to have grown up in Johnstown, Pennsylvania. Our shared culture included a keen work ethic, a participative affiliation with a church, and strong family ties. I knew few really nasty kids, but one is worth mentioning, as he became the centerpiece of one of my father's lessons.

I met Mario in grade school and he came from a family similar to mine. His family also owned a small business; our mothers had known each other for many years. He was a nice kid and was much like every other youngster who attended my school. As he matured, he became more rebellious and prone to getting into trouble. By the eighth grade he was hanging around with some disreputable guys a few years older than we were. He also let his hair grow longer than the average kid and wore clothes that communicated he was taking a path different from most of us.

His mother admitted to my mom that her son's behavior was upsetting their home and that they were worried about him. My mother asked me about the kid's problem. I told her that he was hanging out with a bunch of troublemakers.

In the tenth grade at the Fall Dance, Mario was caught outside the gym smoking and drinking a beer with his older buddies. He was in hot water. Our no-nonsense football coach, who was chaperoning that evening, apprehended the boys. At the urging of his "friends," Mario began to give the coach a hard time. The coach took no bull from any kid and called the police. Mario's "friends" ran into the night, abandoning him, and he was hauled off in the paddy wagon alone.

Mario was disciplined at school for the incident. His parents tried harder than ever to get him under control. My mother spoke pointedly with Mario's mom about the negative impact of his troublemaking friends. The woman assured my mom that her son was really a good boy; it was the influence of rock and roll music, television and movies that was leading him and his buddies astray. The poor kid was the victim of his cultural environment.

The subject of the behavior of my former friend came up at the dinner table one evening. My mom picked up on her friend's story line that rock and roll music, TV and the movies were leading the poor boy astray. "Isn't it a shame what the world is coming to?" she said. Dear old Dad did not buy that excuse and immediately began presenting his counterpoint.

That evening we were having applesauce as part of our meal. Pointing to the applesauce on the table, he asked me, "What does that look like?" I told him, "Applesauce." He then asked my brother Sammy, "What does that smell like?" Sammy said, "It smells like applesauce." Dad turned to our sister, Dolly and said, "Bring me a spoonful of that stuff." When he tasted it he said, "No doubt about it, it is applesauce." I often delighted in my father's lead-ins to "The Message of the Day." The old boy was in top form that evening.

My father had a good neighborhood intelligence network and consequently some insight into the situation. He made it clear to all his children that the boy had made a bad choice of friends. The kid looked like his thug friends, acted like them, and had adopted their outlook on life. Dad made it clear that it had nothing to do with rock and roll music, TV or the movies and everything to do with choices.

"While the boy's mother thinks he is a good kid, he is nothing of the sort," my father said. Looking at each of us he continued, "There are few angels in the company of hoodlums. If you select hoodlums for your friends, look like a hoodlum, and act like a hoodlum, then you are likely a hoodlum yourself, and you had better be prepared to pay the price. If you are intent on acting stupid, you better be tough because the outcomes are not going to be pleasant.

"There is nothing good that can come from a group of thugs all acting and thinking alike. They reinforce their improper behavior and accordingly make poor group choices. Responsible behavior, on the other hand, is never dependent on consensus of opinion. Remember this," he continued, "If it looks, smells, and tastes like applesauce, it is applesauce. You stay away from those kinds of kids; sooner than later they will be making license plates for a living *[READ: working in prison]*." This discussion was clearly a preemptive strike on his part to alert us to choose the proper friends.

The logic of my father's comments was irrefutable. We all promised to sign up to the applesauce test and we did well in that regard. We were given full latitude to choose our friends. My close friends during my teenage years had the same virtue base as I did. If one guy came up with a stupid idea, there were always a few other guys there with cooler heads to keep things under control. We did well because we looked out for one another, although we would never admit that to anyone.

As close as my parents got to managing my friends was an occasional comment from my mother asking if so-and-so was my friend. So-and-so was usually a budding ne'er-do-well; Mother was sending a gentle warning to keep my distance.

Actually, she did get involved when I completed grade school and advanced to the seventh grade at Garfield Junior High School. She arranged with Mrs. Hess, wife of the preacher at the nearby Church of the Brethren, to have her son who was in the tenth grade stop by our home each morning so I could walk to school with him. Walking to school with Cecil was fun. He quickly taught me how to get along at Garfield Junior High School. He was a good person with a wonderful sense of humor and I treasured his friendship.

Cecil never abandoned me. Once, two guys got into a fight in the gym before classes started in the morning. We were close by when it broke out. Cecil grabbed me as the fight began to spread and we exited quickly. He was a true friend; he was intent on delivering me from evil.

As a child and teenager I had many friends who were adults. Among the number were older cousins, uncles, aunts and close family friends. They were always there to add a bit of mature wisdom, serve as my advocate or as a sounding board when I did not want to take an issue to my parents.

My dearest relative friend was my Uncle Joe. He was married to my mother's sister, Sara. Uncle Joe was my attorney in the family court of appeals and was always working a case for me. For example, I had a bad, and unwarranted, reputation for beating up on my younger brother. Sammy was a bright, quiet and devious kid. Often, while reading on his bed, with me far across the room he would, without warning, begin crying and screaming. "Don't hit me, Joe. Ouch! Ouch! You dirty rat, stop it..." On and on it would go.

Let me advise the reader that Sammy's eye never left the page of his *Captain Marvel* comic book during these performances. When he heard my parents coming up the stairs, he would stop yelling and say loudly, "OK Joe, Mom and Dad are coming." When they arrived in the room, Mom would attend to Sammy's recently self-pinched red arm while I received a butt chewing for striking my defenseless, sweet younger brother. After our parents departed, he would get back on the bed, pick up his comic book, look at me and smile. Victory was his one more time.

Overnighting at Uncle Joe and Aunt Sara's home, Sammy started up with the "Don't hit me, Joe" routine. Uncle Joe came up the stairs very quickly and quietly. He stood in the doorway while Sammy was reading his comic book and screaming like a stuck pig. Caught red-handed, Sammy sung like a canary about his previous exploits. Uncle Joe cleared my name when he advised my parents of Sammy's perfidy. After that, I could bop that kid anytime I wanted and get away with it.

Uncle Joe held the same high standards as my Dad; he was equally caring and understanding. I could complain to him without concern and ask his advice and counsel when I did not want to address my father. Uncle Joe was my advocate and my trusted friend; he moved in our family's higher circle.

Joe Taranto was my Dad's longtime friend and associate; he was my closest non-relative, adult friend. For all my teenage years he gave me two dollars every week for spending money. He knew that other kids were not working every day after school. He went out of his way to give me an incentive above my father's weekly pay.

I liked to dress well for school but my father's idea of fashion was limited to bargain basement sales at the Penn Traffic Department Store. At the beginning of my senior year in high school I saw a preppie sport coat in a men's clothing store and spoke to my father about buying it when Joe happened to be present. My Dad's reaction was, "If you can afford it, buy it." Joe was a classy dresser and he could see my disappointment when I responded that buying it would eat too deeply into my college fund savings. My father was pleased to see that I had my priorities straight.

The next Saturday evening there was a high school football game and I planned to go right after work. As often happened, on those nights when I wanted to do something, we worked late. I was hurrying to close the place when Joe asked me to go to his car and bring him the box in the back seat. He told me he had purchased a sport coat the week before. But after he had worn it, he didn't like it. He thought perhaps I could use it, if it fit. When he opened the box there was my preppie sport coat still wrapped in tissue from the store. I thanked him profusely but he waved my appreciation off saying he was glad that he had someone who could fit into his "used" clothes. The jacket fit like a glove and I wore it to the game that evening. Joe was a trusted friend and his circles of influence spread outside our family. I kept him in my information loop. He made sure I did not do anything stupid; he cared for me like an older brother.

My friends of all ages have had a major role in shaping my life. I have learned and benefited from most of them. They kept me on the straight path when it was my inclination to do otherwise. They were kind when it was my intention to be a wise guy. They comforted me when I was feeling down. Their advice and counsel has been of great value. A young man really needs that sort of responsible friendship. Hopefully, I have given something back by being a friend to others. Friends from a spectrum of ages are not only beneficial, but also essential because of their differing perspectives and virtues.

My father's comment that hooligans often restrict their circle of friends to those who think exactly as they do is a valid observation. They don't want a dissenting opinion when making choices. If you are a member of a group bound together by negative groupthink, you are not among friends. When times get tough, you will be abandoned. It is every man for himself. Negative groupthink is to be avoided, as you will most likely do something with others you will not be proud of in the light of day.

Good friends care about you in every regard; they will grow with you, forgive your dumb mistakes, and help you make the right choices when you come to a fork in the road. You will *never* be abandoned.

Time and commitment are the two basic coefficients in the friendship equation. That is, you must spend time together to build trust, confidence and commitment to look out for each other. If either component is missing or you are unwilling to cheerfully provide those components, you don't have a friend; most likely you have only an acquaintance. Having a trusted friend makes the journey through life easier than going it alone.

As a young man I was much like a tightrope walker. Fortunately, I had not one but multiple safety nets under me until I learned to walk the rope with understanding and confidence. My friends, young and not so young, manned those safety nets and all were intent on insuring my personal wellbeing until I was sufficiently competent to address life's challenges on my own. It requires good friends to keep an enthusiastic young man out of trouble. I was blessed in my choice of friends. They were rich in character and gifted with good judgment.

Choose your friends as carefully as you choose your medical doctor. It is really that important.

CHAPTER ELEVEN

MEDICINE MONEY

Preparation and Organization

In addition to many pleasant things in life, we are also regularly confronted with dysfunction, conflict and malicious intent. Being aware of the world around you and then preparing and organizing to respond to potential troublesome situations is essential for your wellbeing as well as that of your family and friends. Without a sense of organization and preparation to deal with life's unexpected events, the probability of being swept away by even a small dysfunctional occurrence is significant. Keep your personal antenna tuned in to the world around you and prepare and organize for contingencies.

My father often told me how the money earned at the family barbershop in Minersville was brought home to Cambria City, a west end suburb of Johnstown in the early 1920's. The punch line that accompanied this story was that they were never robbed walking home because they were prepared and organized. My father firmly believed that preparation and organization were essential to the effective management of the imperfections of daily life.

The Robbery Prevention story goes like this: At the end of each day the contents of the cash register were placed in a vest that my then six-year-old father wore. He had a jacket over the vest and a coat over the jacket. He was unarmed. But Uncle Charlie, Dad's older brother, carried a club and Grandfather Laposata carried a loaded pistol in his hand in a coat pocket. They moved out convoy style from the shop with Uncle Charlie in the lead. Dad followed a few steps directly behind him. In the rear, keeping his eye out for anything unusual, Grandfather covered the convoy with the pistol. The deal was that should any attempt be made to rob them, Dad was to take off for the house, about five blocks from the shop, screaming at the top of his lungs, with Uncle Charlie running interference, brandishing the club. Grandfather would shoot it out with the bad guys as required. Regretfully, I never knew Grandfather Laposata except by reputation; he died three months after I was born.

To get from the barbershop to Cambria City, it was necessary to cross the bridge over the Conemaugh River. Because victims could be isolated on the span and easily sealed off, it was the most dangerous part of the trip home. To test their tactics of bridge crossing, Grandfather Laposata conducted a dry run attack on the bridge one Sunday with Uncle Pete acting as the aggressor. My Dad said that he was almost captured by Uncle Pete on the bridge but managed to escape because he was small and fast. He said that crossing the bridge was really scary because he had little maneuver room on the span and feared being thrown into the river if captured. He noted that he always said a "Hail Mary" upon leaving the shop.

"Life," Dad often related, "was a lot like bringing home the money from the barbershop." There is plenty of good in this world but danger and evil were around the corner.

With some daily thought about matters of preparation and organization, the security and well-being of the family could be maintained.My father often postulated that I was unfamiliar with life's unpleasant side and quite unprepared to deal with it. When I was about fifteen years old Dad set about to change this.

One evening, as we were finishing supper, my father said that a man was coming to see him that evening and that I should sit in the room with him as they spoke. I was to say nothing and show no emotion. My task was to observe. He noted, however, that there would be a discussion after the visit. At the appointed hour, the man arrived. His name was Phil and I recognized him as the husband of Nancy, my mother's friend. My mother and the younger kids quickly evacuated the kitchen. When the man was invited to sit, he glared at me with a GEDOUTTAHERE look. My father, never one to lose his cool, said to him, "The boy is going to stay, pay no attention to him."

My father asked Phil why he had come to see him. He also poured him a glass of wine. Phil drank it in one big gulp and told my father this story. He said that his wife was sick and required medicine. He wanted to buy the medicine but he didn't have enough money to pay for it. Since Nancy was my mother's close friend, she was certain that if Phil came to my father, a generous man who respected his wife's friends, he would lend him the money. The man was clearly nervous telling his story. My father listened in silence and poured the man another glass of wine.

Dad said that my mother had spoken to him of the situation and asked him to help with the purchase of the medicine. Phil fingered the wine glass with anxiety; his face was tight with expectation. My father said, "Out of respect for my wife and her friend, I will give you the money for the medicine." Dad asked him how much money he needed. Before answering, Phil gulped down the second glass of wine.

He grunted out that he needed ten dollars. His facial expression communicated relief as my dad went for his wallet.

Although my father had not initiated any discussion concerning repayment, Phil quickly offered that he would see my father on payday with the ten dollars. He also began to say a lot of nice things about my dad. The Old Boy poured him one more glass of wine, looked him in the eye and said, "My wife will call your wife in an hour to be certain she has taken her medicine. Mary is sincerely concerned about your wife's wellbeing." Phil said he was going directly to the drug store and then to his home. He gulped his third glass of wine, got up, put on his coat, said, "Thanks, Joe," and left our home.

My Dad had me sit next to him and said, "Tell me what you think happened here." When I recalled the story, exactly as Phil had given it to my father, Dad put his head in his hands and said some unflattering things about my powers of observation and my naiveté. He asked, "Did you see how nervous he was?"

I said, "Sure, but people get anxious when they ask for money." His head went back into his hands. Ever patient, he noted that the man literally chug-a-lugged three glasses of wine. "Did that set any bells off in your head?" I confessed that it did not. "Phil was not an Italian and probably doesn't know how to handle a glass of wine," I guessed.

He asked if I had even thought about questioning the amount of money the man requested. "Why would he ask for more than he needed?" I asked. At this point, my father began to speak to himself in Italian; I thought perhaps he was praying.

Then he gave me his take on the meeting. The man had a good job in the steel mill, meaning he had an ample income. Before Phil's arrival, he had made a quick check with his two friends who owned taverns down the street. He found that Phil had an unpaid tab in one bar and regularly stopped for a nightcap in the other. Dad said that he offered the wine to be certain that this man had an affection for alcohol and when he gulped the wine, his suspicions were confirmed. Since my mother had interceded for her friend in some detail he knew the name of the medicine required. To validate the cost of the prescription, he had called his friend who owned the drug store up the street and found that the price was eight dollars. "Why did the man ask for more than he needed?" he asked me.

Getting into the game, I said, "I guess to pay off part of his bill at Nick's Tavern." My father made one of those unintelligible Italian sounds accompanied by hand and arm signals that assured me that I was finally getting a handle on this business. He made sure I understood that Phil's situation was of his own making. He was unprepared to buy the medicine for his wife's sudden illness because of the cost of his drinking habit. Further, he was living week-to-week and had not organized a savings plan to cover the unexpected family expenses. The man was neither prepared nor organized to deal with his family's minor crisis. Phil was reduced to asking my father for aid. "Begging," Dad said, "has a way of diminishing a man's dignity."

To make sure that the man did not stop for a drink on the way home, he had my mother call her friend within the hour. Her husband received my father's message, loud and clear. He had picked up the medicine and had hustled home. She had already taken the first pill when my mom called. Phil dutifully came by the next payday to repay the loan.

My Dad kept me in the information loop on this situation. He told me that he had spoken to Phil about saving a few dollars for emergencies and moderating his drinking when he paid back the money. In short order, Phil paid off his bill at the tavern and was drinking less. Dad was hopeful that he had learned a lesson. In a negative situation of the man's own making, Dad permitted Phil to retain his dignity while repairing the situation but he would not tolerate the man playing him for a fool. The man understood.

I saw Phil at Dad's funeral. Kneeling in prayer at my father's coffin, he was crying like a baby. Later, when we spoke, he recalled that evening in our kitchen and said that my father had changed his life.

I was to sit in on a number of these sessions with my dad. I never spoke but learned a lot. Eventually, I developed Dad's "Prepare and Organize" concept into a credo for my personal and professional life. It has served me well. Although I was never able to see the dark side of life as clearly as my father, I realized that as a six year old, I had never walked home in a convoy, wearing a money vest, accompanied by a club-wielding brother and a pistol-toting father.

Being prepared and organized to deal with issues that arise in daily life is a matter that tests the strength of one's character. It would be nice if life were completely a goodness and love event; but it's not. It is an act of irresponsibility to put one's head in the sand, hoping to avoid the reality of dysfunction, conflict and evil. It is, in fact, a recipe for suffering and anguish when the unprepared and disorganized are confronted with the cruel reality of troublesome situations.

Good judgment, as a character trait, is often the result of being organized and prepared. Good judgment flows from a broad and detailed knowledge of a situation, fermenting in an open mind. Bias and prejudice are natural enemies of good judgment. Spend the time to gather and understand all the facts bearing on an issue before you decide on a course of action. Dad did his homework before handing over the ten dollars.

We have an obligation to assist those who are seemingly unwilling or perhaps unable to prepare and organize. While the unprepared must retain their dignity in the process of being assisted, a firm and responsible effort to modify the behavior that got them into the predicament must accompany your aid. It will take a personal sacrifice on your part to participate in this process. Frustration may be your companion, but you will feel great satisfaction when someone unprepared converts, understands the wisdom of your responsible compassion and changes his ways.

One relaxes in the intellectual contentment that comes when one is free from evading fear of the unknown. Look life squarely in the eye, prepare and organize for probable current and future events... It is a super choice.

CHAPTER TWELVE

WHY DON'T YOU GO TO THE WOODSHOP?

Prejudice Has No Redeeming Qualities

The products of prejudice are without virtue. They dismiss an individual's personal talent, experience and character, pillaging the individual's contribution to himself, his family and our culture. Prejudicial behavior can and must be managed.

Since education was a major issue with my parents and grandparents, I never doubted that I would attend college. They had no firsthand knowledge of the process of advanced education; they only knew that an education was required if one was to prosper in the United States. While they were firm in the belief that I should have the opportunity to attain that education, I would have to depend on the public school system to guide me through the maze.

In the Johnstown school system, students were required to declare a specific course of study beginning in the ninth grade. Every student had a one-on-one meeting with the guidance counselor late in the eighth grade to make his or her declaration. There were three choices: the College Preparatory Course, the Commercial Course and the Manual Arts Courses.

Our family dined together every evening. Actually, considering my father's family management style, dinner was more of a staff meeting with good food. When Dad was finished with his comments, we all spoke during the meal about our issues of interest. If one of us was quiet, we were gently prodded by Mother to speak on some topic. Because the dining table was such a warm and friendly place, conversation came easy for me. I advised my parents at dinner one evening that the date was approaching when I would be required to commit to a course of study in high school. When my father asked whether I had made a choice, I assured him that I was going to select the College Preparatory Course. He nodded his approval and my mother said something supportive about my course selection.

My session the next week with the guidance counselor was in the late afternoon. After dealing with kids all day, by the time she got to me there was little left in her emotional gas tank; she was working on "empty." The counselor had a form to fill out so she began to bark out the questions. When I delayed answering to be certain I understood her questions, she became upset with me. She had a quota to meet that day; my cautious approach was screwing up the deal. Getting through the demographics, the counselor then asked the all-important question: "College, Commercial, or Manual Arts?" When I said "College," she raised her eyes from the paper, and looked at me for the first time during the interview.

"And just where will you go to college?" she inquired. The honest truth was that I had never thought about that before. I blurted out, "Pitt, Penn State" (they were universities near home), and then, because we were Catholic, I added, "or Notre Dame."

The woman threw her pencil on the desktop, fell back in her chair, and asked, "And just who will pay for all this education?" I told her that my father and I would pay. With that she gave me one of those GEDOUTTAHERE looks. She knew of my Italian heritage and that my father was a small businessman. Her line of questioning then took a different turn. She asked if anyone in my family had attended college. I told her that none had. She asked if I even knew of an "Italian kid" who had attended college. I had to confess that I did not. She asked what made me think that I could graduate from college even if my parents could afford to pay the tuition. I confidently replied, "I think I will graduate from college because my parents will tell me to do it." My answer caused her to go for the jugular.

The counselor then said, "Do you know Luigi Como?" I told her I did. "Do you know what course of study he chose last year?" I knew that he had selected the College Preparatory Course but had transferred at midyear to the woodshop where he was happier. When I told her that, she looked at me with an exhausted expression and asked, "Why don't you go the woodshop now and save me the trouble next year?"

Her prejudice was wrapped in logic so I said, "I would rather go to the print shop. Can you work that out?" A few strokes of the pen, a couple of bangs on the paper with a rubber stamp and I was out of there. I felt as if I had faced a very good pitcher and struck out. Yet, it was done. I would pass the details of the interview to all at dinner that evening.

We had assigned seats for dinner. My father sat at the head of the table and as the eldest, I sat at his right hand. When it was my turn to speak, I advised him of the session with the guidance counselor that afternoon. The more I got into the story, the more crimson his face became. At one point he reached over, gently took my arm, and asked me to repeat what I had just said. Glances between my father and mother were flying like lightning as I continued. When I related the guidance counselor's comment, "Why don't you go to the woodshop now and save me the trouble next year?" he tensed up and pushed his chair away from the table. My mother spoke some gentle words of advice to him but he wasn't listening. When I finished, the outcome was about an 8.6 on the Richter Scale.

My father had a talk about the evils of prejudice and he delivered it again that evening in capital letters. His wrath was directed at the guidance counselor. He was prepared to visit the school the next day and make the correction in the records personally. My mother chased the children out of the kitchen and they spoke privately for a while. Dad was calmer when he told me that I was to arrive at school the next morning when the doors opened. I was to stand by the guidance counselor's door until she arrived. When she did arrive I was to give her a note written in his personal hand.

It said, "I insist that my son be enrolled in the College Preparatory class." It was signed, "Joseph T. Laposata." My father told me that if she said one word, I was to leave the school, come home, get him, and he would go to the school and speak directly with her.

With that he said, "Your mother and I have confidence that you will do well in school. You have the talent, and we will not stand for you to be dealt with unfairly because of this woman's prejudice against people of Italian heritage. Tell me now if you are not motivated to study hard and do well." I assured him that I was properly motivated and that ended the conversation.

I did exactly as my father directed the next morning. When the counselor arrived at her room she was fresher in spirit than the afternoon before. She was surprised to see me and asked if I was waiting for her. I advised her that my father had written a note and handed her the envelope. I told her I was to go home for my father if she had any questions. The counselor read it and immediately understood that she had made an error in the manner she had treated me the day before. She asked me what I had told my father. I related that I told him everything exactly as it had happened.

"I'm sorry for yesterday," she said. "I was tired. You tell your father that I have changed the commitment form to the College Preparatory Course."

And that was the end of it. I entered the college preparatory course in high school and did well. Just as significantly, my father's direct approach in dealing with matters of unwarranted prejudice was locked in my mental hard drive.

From that day forward I remained very sensitive to how others reacted to my Italian heritage. I expected the worst when someone decided to play the "ethnic card." Consequently, I responded to that sort of prejudice with moderated aggression. In my first few days at college I was pleased that ethnic origin was not an issue on campus. However, my antenna was still up and operating; it was a matter of self-defense. As freshman orientation ended, I was called to the Office of the Registrar. The note I received said there was a problem with my "nationality" and that I should report immediately. I went there assuming that I was going to be dismissed because I was an "Italian" so that an American could enter the college in my place. A similar situation had occurred when I was in high school and I was replaced by an American kid in an extracurricular activity. Simply, the kid went home and told his parents he was not selected. The next day a very contrite teacher, after some guidance from above, told me that she had made a mistake, and, rather than selected... I was the first alternate. It was her mistake and she was sorry. Notably, I understood what was really going on.

The college registrar was a gentle woman and very business-like. She had my registration form in her hand. She said, "There is a problem with your registration form. I think we can clear this up quickly with a simple question." I was holding my breath when she asked me where I was born. I told her, "In Johnstown at Mercy Hospital." She then asked why I put "Italian" in the block requesting my nationality. I assured her I did that because I *was* an Italian. This very nice woman softly advised me that since I was born in the United States I was an American. She crossed out "ITALIAN and wrote, "AMERICAN" in the nationality block. Smiling, she reminded me that since I had been born in the USA, I was an American. From that day forward I believed I was an American. The woman's simple assurance that I was really an American produced an epiphany that shook my soul. I realized that while I was most proud of my Italian heritage, to be an American meant that I was equal to everyone else. I never had felt that way when I thought of myself as an Italian. Understanding that simple concept took a chip off my shoulder. When I made the choice to believe I was an American, my life changed for the better.

In thirty-three years of military service I had only one situation of prejudice that caused me to react. In that case it was not my heritage in question, but my religion. Transferred to a new unit, I was introduced with my wife at a large unit welcome party as a "Fish Eater." (Some years ago, Catholics did not eat meat on Fridays and the "Fish Eater" moniker was popular among bigots.) Everyone laughed at the colonel's comment except my wife and me. That was noted by one of the colonel's boys and I was told to "loosen up." The same term was used at a staff call the next week and again at a social that weekend. Each time the colonel used that term, the group laughed on cue. I copied my father's Sicilian glare, and all could see that I wasn't happy. I did not appreciate being treated with what I considered prejudiced disrespect.

On Monday morning I was at the colonel's office under a full head of steam. If this officer was going to disrespect me for my religion, we were going to have other problems.

I wanted to nip it in the bud. The colonel's deputy was a bright guy and kind enough to listen to my story. Wisely, he kept me away from the boss. "No need to self-destruct on this one. Let me handle it," he said. The next day he called and told me that I would never hear the comment again. He was correct; no one ever said that in my presence again.

If that colonel had questioned my ability to do the job assigned, I could have handled it, but a "Fish Eater" was not acceptable. I was an American, a loyal officer in good standing in the United States Army, and my religious affiliation was not part of that equation.

The Army does a marvelous job in managing prejudice. Soldiers are valued for their talent, performance and character. From the short list of reasons why I made the Army my career, freedom from prejudice was one of them. A one-week experience out of thirty-three years of service doesn't give the Army a record of perfect performance, but it is pretty darned close.

My father frequently spoke about choosing virtues over vices. His story line was that if you chose to follow the path of a vice, that path would eventually take you over a cliff. If you chose the path of a virtue you would find a trail with an easy and safe gradient into the valley. The point is that when you willingly accept prejudicial disrespect you are taking the vice trail by lacking the moral courage to stand up for what is proper and just. Matters of prejudice must be promptly and directly addressed.

Those who place people in categories practice a more insidious form of prejudice. The counselor's prejudice put me into the "Italian" category. She expected that I should be satisfied doing something for my life's work that *she* thought Italians were capable of doing. My father's point was that we were not Italians, we were Americans. We were of Italian heritage, but we were citizens, managing businesses, voting and paying taxes. We were caring, contributing, and respected members of our community. He wanted no part of the mindset that put people into diverse groups. It tends to restrain upward mobility, except within the group, and he wanted no part of it.

He said, "We didn't come to America to be Italians living in the United States. We can respect our heritage in our home, but we are Americans living in America." Dad made certain that this lesson of confronting unjust prejudicial behavior was implanted into my brain. In spite of his efforts, I actually believed I was an Italian until I went to college because I was called an Italian and that was the way the institutions outside my family treated me.

My college experience assured me that prejudice could be managed. The Army repeatedly demonstrated that even the behavior of prejudiced individuals could be controlled. Prejudice has no redeeming qualities... Rejecting prejudice is the only choice.

CHAPTER THIRTEEN

ECCLESIASTICAL ENTREPRENEURSHIP

Managing Money

Dishonesty rooted in greed is dysfunctional and will produce unnecessary stress in your life. When your greed is discovered, your anxiety level will be exponentially increased.

Shortly after moving to Oakhurst in 1947, my mother enlisted me as a St. Therese Church altar boy. Our duties consisted of serving daily Mass at 6:00 AM for a week each month, Sunday Mass when directed and weddings and funerals on request.

When I was about fifteen years old, I attended a funeral with my parents at a church in a Johnstown suburb and noticed that after the Funeral Mass, as the people were leaving the church, the two altar boys stood in the rear near the doors, each holding a glass dish. Significantly, people were dropping money in the plates. I made it a point to connect up with one of the altar boys who told me that they split the money collected. He said the nuns felt that since the boys were giving up a good portion of their day to serve, the collection was a small remuneration for their services. I noticed that there were five dollar bills in the plate, plenty of ones and some change. At that point, the "opportunity" light went on in my head and my entrepreneurial spirit kicked in.

I had made a deal with my father that I would establish a savings program with the intent to pay my college tuition. I took the obligation seriously and wanted to be certain that I could begin college with funds sufficient to cover two years' tuition. My goals were well advertised in the family.

Accordingly, I took any job that would produce income. My dear Aunt Sara hired me to cut her grass and overpaid me for my work. Joe Taranto hired me to do small jobs around his home and gave me more money than I deserved. Needing new golf clubs, I was too frugal to spend the money for better clubs. My Uncle Fred, a super guy, gave me his like-new clubs and bought himself a new set.

The newly recognized belief that I could supplement my income and meet my ecclesiastical commitments at the same time set me into action. I went to the nun who was the Chief of Altar Boys and volunteered to serve all funerals and weddings during the summer vacation period. She was thrilled; she thought that she might have a young man on the cusp of priesthood. I did not interrupt that notion by advising her that my true motives were exclusively fiduciary. My father was not thrilled by this move as he wanted me at work in the barbershop where I had a flourishing "Shave" trade. However, he was supportive of the church and gave me his approval.

Weddings were a sell out in late May and June that year. July and August were also nearly all booked. Since we had a young parish, funerals were sparse. I made it a point not to have my assistant altar boys participate in my operation. I swiftly went to the rear of the church after the service with my glass tray, smiling and wishing one and all a long life and happiness, while collecting a pocket full of change and a wad of bills.

Funerals were so sad that I felt a little bad soliciting. However, the tuition train was calling; so I stood quietly with the tray. I had seen my father's system of accounting for income to prepare his taxes so I emulated his process to account for my earnings at the church. My assistants never said anything to me about my "work" at the rear of the church, the priests never really saw me in action and the nuns did not cover weddings and funerals. At one of the last weddings before school began, one of my assistants asked if he could get in on the action at the rear of the church. He was a good kid so I cut him in on the deal. That was a bad choice, as he took his money and flashed it around. When his mother pinned him down concerning the origin of his newfound wealth, he coughed up the story in detail. His mother called my mother and I was on the hot seat...again.

According to my mother it was irrelevant that the altar boys at the other church were pocketing the money. The difference was that they had permission and I was "conducting a solicitation operation using the church as a front." She was embarrassed and horrified by my behavior. She made a quick call to the convent and then seized my account book. In short order we were off to visit the nun who was the Chief of Altar Boys. My mother was certain my salvation was now in question and some reparation was in order.

The nun was much less excited by the situation than my mother. She told my mother that she had heard that I was soliciting tips but felt that because I was doing a good job and was "sacrificing" my work time in the barbershop, she let it go. When my mother produced my account book listing my summer earnings, the nun was visibly shaken. I had earned over $500 and had every penny properly registered in the bank account book. The nun was aware of my commitment to my father to pay for college tuition so she announced a Solomon-like decision to close the issue.

The nun said that while I should have solicited permission to set up shop collecting after weddings and funerals, she admired my dedication to advance my education. Sister made it clear that, while my processes were flawed, my motives mitigated the transgressions. She made it clear that I could keep the $500 and that she would be managing the "solicitation" issue in the future. She told my mother the issue was closed. The nun also recommended a trip to the confessional to speak with the priest who was the Commander of Altar Boys. She personally would brief him on the matter.

My mother told my father of my latest escapade at dinner that evening and he was stunned. "I thought if Joe paid for his education it would mean more to him and motivate him to excel," he said. "Instead, he sets up a front operation at the church to feather his college fund. I should have known that brain of his would get him in trouble. The fault here is as much mine as it is his." Of course, I received the mandatory wisdom lecture from my father, which closed the issue with him.

My mother did not let go easily. My father and I (being the oldest son) were served our meals. For the next few weeks I noted that I was served a lesser cut of meat or a little less dessert or the burnt corner piece of lasagna. Her subtle dissatisfaction with me was noted. I did all I could to get back in her good graces.

The priest did not encourage my going to Confession for this "transgression". He said it was a minor issue. We did have, however, a lengthy man-to-man talk about money, its value in this world, how being obsessed about money could contribute to making poor choices and why I should reassess my fiscal perspectives. He was very helpful in shaping my thoughts. The priests and nuns at our church did their job in promoting religion but their understanding of human nature and its frailties was really impressive. My faith was reinforced by this event. To this day I view money as being essential, but it is not important enough to drive me to do something improper.

I am thankful for this episode in my life. In the long run, the need to collect a fortune from my life's work was a secondary matter to me. If money were really important to me, I would never have joined the Army. My initial pay as a junior officer was about $2,500 per year. My college graduate friends teaching school or entering business were starting between $5,000 and $9,000 per year. I truly served in the Army to support and defend the Constitution of the United States. It sounds rather lofty, but it fit me perfectly.

As a family, Anita, the boys and I lived in genteel poverty until I was a major. Thankfully, things are much better these days for soldiers. However, the St. Therese Wedding and Funeral caper provided me a deeper insight into the accumulation of money.

Of course, Anita and I could have asked our parents to supplement my income in those early years. It was a matter of pride for Anita and me to grow together and to experience a little hardship, as so many of our Army friends did. Make the choice to manage your money effectively, securely and morally. Greed or money ill-gotten will bring only embarrassment and grief.

Chapter Fourteen

Eternal Salvation and Armistice Day

Respect and Honor

Many young men and women in their enthusiasm for life sometimes disrespect people and issues they don't like or don't understand. Education often modifies that behavior and diminishes disrespect and dishonor. Respect for others is the keystone for establishing strong, lasting personal and organizational relationships. The respect you demonstrate for others will be returned to you many times over.

I entered Indiana State Teachers College in Indiana, Pennsylvania as a serious young man. My classmates were largely middle class, second generation Americans. Our parents had endured the Great Depression and World War II, and very few were college educated. Many of us were the first in our families to attend college. Our parents, intent on a better life for us, made a number of personal and financial sacrifices to get us there. We felt a responsibility to excel because we were told, repeatedly, of our great opportunity to be educated. We could not let our families down by squandering the opportunity for advancement.

I found the college course work interesting and challenging; I knew that I would do well. The easiest course that first semester was the Reserve Officer Training Corp (ROTC) class. However, I didn't care about the military, wanted nothing to do with it, and was something of a wise guy in the classroom. ROTC was a mandatory course for two years.

It also was required that freshmen stay on campus for the first few weeks of the school year to become accustomed to the routine of life at the college.

When we were permitted to go home for the weekend, my Uncle Joe and Aunt Sara were there to transport me the thirty miles from Indiana to Johnstown. I had plenty of stories for my parents about my classes and my new friends. When I related my ROTC high jinx (with a little embellishment), I had people holding their sides with laughter.

It had been arranged that we would dine together at my grandparents' home on the Sunday before I returned to college so that I could share my new experiences. Uncles and aunts were also in attendance waiting for an accounting of my collegiate stewardship. As the oldest of my generation, I was the first to do almost everything and received all the adulation – and responsibility - that went with it. Being my parent's "kid development project," I knew that their reputation for properly raising a child was on the line. Sicilians are sensitive to even the slightest signs of weakness. Thus, I was intent on keeping my report upbeat and positive.

My grandfather was a wonderful man and a family patrician, first class. When we arrived at his home he kissed me and said, "We are so happy you are doing well at school. This is why we came to the United States; one generation and we have a boy in college."

When my grandmother kissed me, she held my face in her kind, loving hands and began to weep with happiness. I received the usual razzing from my uncles and supportive praise from my aunts who were my protectors. The meal of fresh, home-prepared food was wonderful and so was the feeling of being surrounded by everyone that I loved. It couldn't get much better until someone said, "Joey, tell them the story of the ROTC class." I proceeded to make a joke out of ROTC, my officer instructors, and the Army in general. My audience was laughing; I was on a roll. However, I did eventually notice that my grandfather was clearly not pleased with my performance. He seemed serious and progressed to anger by the time I was finished. He adjourned the dinner abruptly, and taking my arm, we retired to the parlor. Figuring that something was up, only my dad came into the room with Grandfather and me. Everyone else stayed in the kitchen.

My grandfather had served in the U. S. Army as a Private First Class in World War I in France and was wounded. He was also one of the founding members of Post Number 2 of the Disabled American Veterans (DAV) in Johnstown, Pennsylvania. Notably, he carried the American flag when the DAV marched in local parades. When it came to patriotism, he had few peers.

He got in my face, drill sergeant style, and read me the riot act. He said that I had no right to denigrate the Army. It was the protector of our Republic and was composed of men of courage and high character. He had friends who remained in France after the war, he said. They were buried there in defense of my right to attend college and that I was something of an irresponsible ass to bring dishonor to their sacrifice. "My officers were the most courageous men I have ever known," he said. "They cared for their soldiers before they cared for themselves. They had a burden of responsibility that was extraordinary. You cannot discredit these men in my presence, do you understand?"

Shaken by his aggressive words, I could only weakly reply, "Yes, sir." My adolescent insensitivity to my grandfather's patriotism had me in a hole. I ran up the white flag. By this time the parlor was filled with my grandmother, mother, aunts and uncles all observing the proceedings. Saving me some face, someone had whisked my cousins, brothers and sister out of the house. When my grandfather had finished with me, there was a dead silence and an anticipation of what would come next.

His voice became softer as he said to me, "You and I will attend Holy Mass on Armistice Day, on November 11th. You will wear your ROTC uniform and we will take Holy Communion together. I will contact the college, if necessary, to have you released." I was still shaking in my shoes from his uncharacteristic and unexpected butt chewing. Again, I could only muster a trembling, "Yes, sir."

Now here is the centerpiece of the story. My grandfather was not one to take a slight of disrespect from anyone, not even a priest. A small issue had come up some years before at the church. I never had all the details, but reportedly, my grandfather's affiliation with that institution diminished because of the encounter. In spite of this, he remained a spiritual man while my grandmother was a truly religious person. She followed all the rules of the Church with sincere precision and had been praying for some time for my grandfather to return to the Church, to go to confession, and take Holy Communion. As he was getting along in years, an unexpected call to his heavenly reward was not entirely out of the question.

When Grandfather made this startling commitment to return to church with the caveat that I was to go with him in my uniform, my grandmother, mother, and aunts were convinced that a miracle had occurred. My parents said they would have me home in time for Armistice Day (now Veteran's Day) Mass. Meanwhile my Uncle Sam, a former Marine, and my Uncle Joe, a B-26 Crew Chief during World

War II, assured Grandfather that I would show up properly polished. The matter was now out of my hands. I could see that I was an instrument (READ: pawn) in the hands of a family intent on saving the eternal soul of my grandfather.

In short order, all returned to normal; as normal as could be expected after thanks had been expressed to the Blessed Virgin Mary, Saint Jude, Saint Anthony and a litany of other saints with whom I was unfamiliar. I was kissed and hugged by the women and congratulated by the men for reasons beyond my comprehension. There were, however, two things about which I was very certain: There would be no more loose talk about the Army *and* we were going to church on Armistice Day.

My dad came to the college and picked me up in the evening of November 10th. He said that Uncle Sam and Uncle Joe would be at our home to spit and polish me to perfection. I was to be fully cooperative. There are television shows these days that feature some Plain Jane submitting herself to something called a "makeover." I know exactly how these poor women feel as I was subject to the same experience that evening.

I was given a haircut and then my uncles went to work. When they finished, I looked like General Patton. Yet Mother gave the uniform one last touch up, pressing it while my father reminded me of the seriousness of this matter. I retired to bed uncertain about the morrow.

I have to admit that I felt like a boy in a soldier's costume the next morning. In my father's car I picked up my grandfather at the appointed time. He inspected my uniform, enjoined me to stand very straight, told me he was proud of me, and we took off for church. One must understand that when dealing with a Sicilian, things are never quite what they seem.

I trusted my grandfather completely, but I was smart enough to know that this was not strictly a *sacramental* event. When we departed his home thirty minutes before Mass was to begin, I knew the game was on.

There was a parking space right in front of the church, but my grandfather said, "Don't park there; continue down the street." We were about a block away from the church when I finally pulled the car to the curb. Approaching the church we observed the usual scenario: The women went directly inside while the men loitered outside.

My grandfather was impeccably dressed. He was wearing a gray double-breasted suit with a brilliant white shirt and an Italian silk tie. As we were making our final approach he said to me, "Let's get in step. We want to look good when we arrive."

The men in their small groups stopped talking; some threw their cigarette butts away as all eyes turned to my grandfather and me. It was a martial entrance akin to an honor guard arriving. They knew something was up, and they were about to witness it firsthand.

My grandfather was my height and truthfully, we cut a fine figure together. I was wearing my dad's skintight, black Italian gloves because it was chilly. I glistened and shone from my shoes to the brass on my hat. We walked up to a man who was selling red poppies. My grandfather bought two flowers.

One he carefully placed on the left breast pocket of my uniform and the other on his suit lapel. The seller respected my grandfather and spoke to him with deference.

We approached the first group of men outside the church, all of whom, like us, were wearing poppies. Each man spoke to my grandfather with the utmost of respect. Of course there was some anticipation to know who I was. My grandfather said, "This is my grandson, Joseph. He is studying biology in college and he is going to be an Army officer." I wanted to advise them I had no intention of becoming an officer, but wisely I kept my mouth shut and maintained that all-business look that my grandfather had perfected. I greeted the men in turn and shook their hands.

One old man looked at me closely, examining every detail of the uniform with his eyes, touched the lapels of the coat and said, in a tone of reverential disbelief, "An officer." I realized in an instant that it was the uniform that was the object of their respect: I was being honored and respected because I had the right to wear that special piece of clothing and all that it represented. Immediately, I followed my grandfather's lead. I was not about to disgrace that uniform. I stood straight; I was respectful as I spoke about the sacrifice of those who died and remained in a cemetery in France. My grandfather proudly introduced me to every man standing in front of the church.

There was a signal from an usher and the men quickly filed into the church. My grandfather said, "Let's allow everyone to enter, then we will go in." The church was packed and I could not see an available seat. My grandfather said, "Now, let's march to the front pew like soldiers." Our conspicuous presence was impossible to ignore as we proceeded down the aisle. When we arrived at the front of the church there were two vacant seats on the aisle in the front row. We were seated and the priest entered the altar. It occurred to me that they were waiting for us and that the seats were reserved.

My grandfather took my hand during the sermon as we listened to the priest extolling the virtues of service to our Republic. When it was time for Holy Communion, we marched to the rail, took the host, and when we returned to our seats, Grandfather took my hand again and looked into my eyes with an expression that is still locked into my soul. We seemed to communicate for a moment on a level higher than words. In an instant I understood my grandfather, as a person, and what he wanted me to do with my life. Silently, by taking his hand, I tried to communicate that I understood what he wanted and that I would do my best.

After Mass we met at my grandparents' home for coffee and Italian pastries. We did not speak of what had just happened but embraced the goodness of our lives and the comfort of our mutual affection. Returning home, I was quickly transported back to Indiana, Pennsylvania and was in my dormitory room by three o'clock that afternoon. It took me a while to understand all that had happened that day, but I knew that my life had changed forever. Notably, deep in my heart, I felt that I was going serve as an Army officer.

Now, for some advice: First, it is prudent to control your scorn. Denigrating individuals, institutions, policies, and so on is unwarranted and your lack of insight will be quickly countered by rational opposing arguments. Looking foolish is a probable outcome. Presenting a contrasting point of view is an entirely different issue when done in a thoughtful, dignified manner but respect and honor are absent when one is knifing an adversary in the back with words.

Second, observe from this story how my grandfather created a situation to teach me the essential nature of respect and honor. By making these qualities the centerpiece of a human drama, he had branded the virtue of those character traits into my being. By showing that he could overcome his own issues with an institution to teach me a lesson enhanced the impact. Skillfully weaving my adolescent disrespect for the Army into an experience that gave direction to my professional life was his stroke of genius.

He understood that it is common for young people, in their enthusiastic but myopic view of life, to feel that respect is something to be disrespected. He allowed that disrespect is a behavior to be experienced but must be quickly put away for more responsible deportment as an adult. Grandfather took immediate corrective action and gave me the opportunity to *experience* the virtues of respect and honor first hand, an experience that motivated me to understand and change my ways. Words alone were insufficient to drive this point home. I suspect that I am not alone in this sort of epiphany.

As a final note, if one serves in the military, the issue of respect for the uniform is a matter of paramount importance. That apparel represents the many men and women who have previously worn the uniform and served with honor. It is even a greater sign of respect for those who have made the supreme sacrifice defending our Constitution. The uniform is almost a sacred vestment in our Republic. It represents the best of its citizens. It must be worn with pride and dignity; the ghostly spirit of the Soldiers, Sailors, Airmen, and Marines who have gone before you will buoy you up to a higher standard.

Choose to respect and honor family, friends, acquaintances and even strangers. It is the higher path. Make this choice early in life, as it is a foundation for establishing good interpersonal relationships.

CHAPTER FIFTEEN

YOU GOTTA FEEL IT IN YOUR GUT

The Sixth Sense

Intuition is defined as a "sense of something not evident." Most of us have had an experience where we have had an intuitive feeling about a situation that suggests we take a certain action for our safety, security or wellbeing. In our professional and personal lives a sensitized intuition is a valuable gift. It promotes making pertinent and wise decisions at home and in the workplace that contribute to positive outcomes for yourself, your family and your colleagues.

In matters of family management my father was very traditional. However, when it came to business, he was quite flexible. When he was certain that change was required, he adapted and stayed in tune with the desires of our customers. Business rules were never chipped into stone tablets. I've observed that successful businessmen are generally of a liberal mentality. Inflexible, unimaginative, "do-it-by-the-book" types may do well in the short run but they often wilt in the marathon.

My father believed the Army was a rigid, doctrinal organization inhabited by obedient automatons. Notably, he was very wrong on that one. When it became clear I planned to select a career in the military, he set about to advise me on the negative aspects of the Army's mentality and the goodness of his capitalistic credo.

Dad was inducted into the Army in World War II but was rejected because of a problem with his right eye. His military experience was vicarious; he got an earful from talkative customers who served in World Wars I and II as well as Korea. To this end, Dad enlisted his best friend, John, a World War I veteran, to share his impressions of the Army with me. John was a man of extraordinary perspective possessing an intellect that was without bias or prejudice. He could see logic and truth through clouds of confusion and deceit. He had thoughts on almost everything and spoke in a straightforward, easy-to-understand manner. John was a Polish immigrant, had only a grade school education, but was the wisest man in our neighborhood. Since he visited our home a couple of nights a week, an arrangement was made for him to transfer his wisdom concerning the Army to me.

He started our session by telling me he was "only a private first class and a motorcycle messenger," but he had seen enough to give me some solid advice. He began with a story about a company commander who was a military school graduate. According to John, this man applied extraordinarily high standards during their initial training in France. He graphically described the man's brutality in enforcing those standards, his administrative brilliance, and his tactical incompetence in training. The man led by rigidly following doctrine and orders rather than making an assessment of the situation and modifying the plan as required. He was incapable of improvising, and when required to innovate, he usually fell apart under the weight of decision-making. John said that it was obvious to the rank and file that this officer was going to get people killed in combat. "He was somebody's favorite and they kept him in command," he said. "They were going to allow him to prove his incompetence at the soldiers' expense." The first time the unit came under enemy fire the captain quickly went down, shot in the leg by a German machine gunner. There was a story of his valor, a medal was presented, he was put into the hospital to recover and then assigned to a desk job where he would not get anyone hurt, including himself.

"The good leaders we had were men of character. They had the special quality of being able to do the right things at the right time. They pushed us hard, they endured our hardships, they knew when enough was enough, and when more was REALLY required," he said.

He went on, "Officers must have common sense; even more than that, they must have an intuitive feeling about the situation. I don't mean that they have to be crystal ball readers, but they have to be informed, observant, and tuned in to all that is going on around them. The good officers always seemed to know what was right, took action when it was required, and didn't do stupid things; we trusted them with our lives."

"Most were not career officers. They were not brilliant men, but they were savvy and clear-thinking men. They were not great tacticians, but they knew enough to capitalize on the Germans' weaknesses and to avoid their strong points. They cared for their soldiers but not so caring that they allowed us to get soft. What set these officers apart from others was their intuition. They had a sixth sense about where to go, what to do, how to do it, and what to expect from the Germans. If you must go into the Army, be that kind of officer and you will earn the respect and admiration of your soldiers." He was quick to add that developing that sixth sense would not be found by reading a book. "Intuition," he said, "is something you gotta feel in your gut. Some have it and some are never going to have that gift."

At the end of the discussion I told John and my dad that I really wanted to give the Army a try. The ROTC officers I knew were honorable men and I trusted them. I promised John and Dad that I would stay intellectually flexible, that I would never misuse my authority, and would try to be, in John's words, "firm, but fair." Lastly, I was uncertain about intuition, but would not forget about it and do my best to develop some.

This conversation is etched into my memory because John finished by saying, "Joseph, you can be a good officer if you pay attention to these simple thoughts. Execute your responsibilities as best you can and be a man of moral character like your father." John's words even seemed to have an effect on my dad. He appeared to better understand my choice of a career even though he didn't like it.

A few weeks later, my father asked me to represent him at a ward-level, Democratic Party fundraising dinner. He had purchased a ticket but decided that he would rather stay at home that evening. I regularly substituted for my father and actually enjoyed going to church, political, social and community affairs in his place. The food at political party dinners was never all that good and this one was no exception. After the last rousing speech about the goodness of the Democratic party, they had a few prizes to raffle off. One prize was a case of Rolling Rock beer and I had the winning ticket. As I went forward to claim my loot, someone yelled, "Hey, that's Joe Laposata's kid." By the time I arrived at the head table it was noted that I was not yet twenty-one years old and could not be given the beer.

The Master of Ceremonies was a funny guy and said some cute things about the party not wanting to contribute to the delinquency of a minor. That short delay gave me the opportunity to gather my thoughts. With some seriousness and in a stern voice, I said that I wanted to be certain that I fully understood the situation. That is, the beer was won by my father's ticket but it could not be given to me, his legal representative, because I was not of drinking age in the Great State of Pennsylvania. This seemed to sober everyone up a bit; the room went silent. While uncertain where I was going with this, the head table crew held firm their position: "No beer for the kid."

I then said, with some bravado, while pointing the mandatory index finger skyward, "In that case, acting on behalf of my father, I direct the Master of Ceremonies to give twelve bottles of my father's beer to Father Bede." The priest was a popular fellow in our end of town and was the chaplain that evening at the head table. The Master of Ceremonies came to attention, and marching to the head table like a soldier, placed the twelve bottles of beer in front of the smiling priest as if they were candles on the altar. The dinner attendees were laughing at the Master of Ceremonies' antics. When he reported back to me, the crowd went silent again.

I directed the next six bottles be given to our "distinguished Ward Chairman." There was lots of applause and shouts of "Atta boy, Joey." The bottles were delivered with mock solemnity. When the Master of Ceremonies reported to me that there were still six bottles remaining, his eyebrows went up and a big smile crossed his face. He did everything except say, "Give me the beer." I pretended, just for an instant, to study the situation and then said with a flourish and a wave of the hand, "The remaining six bottles of my father's beer are to be given to our capable Master of Ceremonies." With that, he ran to the beer case, opened a bottle and drank it down to the delight of everyone in the hall.

There was a pandemonium of laughter. The meeting was adjourned and on the way out of the hall, folks said kind things to me and most noted that, I was "a chip off the old block." On the way home I decided not to discuss the "Great Beer Giveaway" with my dad. It was just a little more good-time foolishness on my part.

When I got home, my mother was reading the newspaper at the kitchen table. She smiled and said, "Your father is on the back porch." (Translation: The old boy wants to see you.) Dad was smoking a Parodi cigar and sitting on the swing. He had me sit with him and said, "How was the dinner?" I told him it was the usual stuff and then I told him some of the highlights of the speeches. "Did they raffle off any prizes?" he said. I looked at him and said, "I guess you heard what happened." It was only a twenty-minute walk home but Johnny, who owned the gas station up the street, called my dad and filled him in on the details before I could reach home. News traveled quickly in Johnstown.

My father was stingy with praise but he put his arm around me and said, "I am proud of you. What made you do that?" I told him, "It seemed like the thing to do at the time. The Master of Ceremonies was so funny; it was sort of an improvised skit that we made up as we went along. I knew you would not miss the beer and I was certain I was doing something good." He paused for a moment and made a statement that was very important to me. "You know," he said, "just maybe you do have a little of my intuition in your blood." My mother came out to the porch, kissed me, and spoke kind words of praise for my actions. I tried to understand what "intuition" had to do with my actions that evening, but I was now sure that I had "it" and slept well.

When my dad and John made me aware of the sixth sense of intuition, I really didn't understand the concept. It has taken me a number of years but now I can at least write a simple statement of how it works with me. Speaking only for myself, I find that the broader my experience in personal and professional matters, the greater my contact with people of different perspectives, the broader my education and training, the better functioning my intuitive skills become. It is almost like the hard drive in my brain has stored and cataloged information from all my life experiences and held it in file. When I was presented with an issue, my resident search engine scanned all the appropriate files in my "little gray cells" and produced a feeling about how to deal with the issue as well as options for positive outcomes. It seems to happen as fast in the brain as it does in any online search engine on my computer. I know that this sounds unscientific but that is how intuition seems to work with me; others advise that it works the same way for them.

I suggest you make the choice to expand your intuitive skills by growing intellectually and by meaningful personal and professional experiences. Remove all bias and prejudice from your mind. Load up your factory-installed hard drive (READ: Your brain), relax and let it do the rest. I suspect we all have the gift of a sixth sense; we just must make the choice to develop it.

Choosing to develop this gift will ease and embellish the execution of your professional and personal responsibilities. Listen to that little voice in your head after you have considered all the facts bearing on a problem; a functioning sixth sense will contribute to your life's achievements and successes. Choosing to develop your sixth sense is hard work but the positive outcomes it produces confirm it to be a wise choice...in both the workplace and at home.

Chapter Sixteen

You Can Be President

Management of Aspirations and Expectations

Most of us have seen a situation where a person has a burning aspiration to achieve an important goal in life. The individual has worked hard, is at the cusp of success, and fully expects that the aspiration will be achieved. Then, for whatever reason, the person fails or perceives failure to achieve that goal and falls into a debilitating depression. Managing your aspirations and expectations can minimize the effects of a negative outcome. Do not permit yourself to be killed by your dreams.

I attended both the Defense System Management College (DSMC) and the Industrial College of the Armed Forces (ICAF). Each course was a marvelous academic and professional experience. The courses of study were challenging. I took the time to read extensively. Every day brought a new revelation about management of my personal and professional life. I grew by leaps and bounds while under the care of the superb faculties at these highly valued institutions. The concept of managing one's aspirations and expectations as expressed in this story is a collage of inputs coming from a variety of personal readings, course work and guest speakers at DSMC/ICAF.

Significantly, choosing to manage aspirations and expectations required the wisdom of not only my military elders but also my familial elders. This issue is so simple and straightforward that I considered not including it in this compendium. Yet, its importance in my life was so significant that I am compelled to offer it for your consideration.

When I was a child, my grandfather often told me that I could be President of the United States. He ensured that I knew the opportunity to be upwardly mobile was uniquely an American condition and was not to be squandered. It was my birthright to have the opportunity to rise to the highest office in the government of our Republic.

He also advised me that America was the proponent of individual rights, not group rights and privileges as in the "old country." Grandfather stressed that in America I was limited only by my determination to excel.

My attendance at college was viewed as a positive first step towards my attaining what he hoped would be my life's work. It is important to note that the word "work" as used here did not just mean "labor," but rather connoted a person's contribution to the greater American culture and society.

During my first year at college, my grandfather said he would like to visit the campus to spend a day there with me to better understand my academic and personal lifestyle. It was during the spring of my freshman year that we arranged a Saturday visit.

We departed Johnstown early in the morning and drove to Indiana, Pennsylvania in my dad's car. There were plenty of students on campus for "background" effect as I gave him a complete tour to include my dorm room, which had been appropriately prepared for inspection. We walked through classrooms and laboratories and he got a view of my fraternity house. He was uncertain about fraternities and wanted my assurance that they were not secret societies like some in Italy. He relaxed when I told him that a fraternity was a social club...and mine was filled with some of the best men on campus.

He really liked the college bookstore and the Student Union. In fact, we ate lunch at the Union and I introduced him to every friend that passed by. He took special interest in the library and we stayed there for a long time. Before returning home we walked through the town and had our evening meal in an Italian restaurant. During the meal he asked what I intended to do with my life. Did I aspire to be an Army Officer? A college professor? Perhaps a doctor?

"When one lives in a wonderful country like the United States, its citizens have an obligation to repay the nation for its many gifts." He said, "I cheerfully pay taxes for the privilege of living in the United States. But it goes one step further; it would be a noble thing and bring honor to our family if you served our country with your intellect and enthusiasm. You have more talent than you realize, Joey. Do not aspire to small things. With your enthusiasm and all this opportunity, good things will come to you." Never wishing to offend or disappoint him, I told my grandfather that I still had a long way to go at college and that doing well, every day, was my goal. Later on, if the opportunity to enter a career of service to the country presented itself, I would certainly consider it.

Therein lies the first premise of managing aspirations and expectations. Mine were focused on achieving well-defined, near-term goals that I could manage on a daily basis. In short, I believed that if I set many short term goals and did them all to the point of excellence, these smaller attainments would combine to produce a broader perspective of my achievement and potential. All of these well-defined, near-term tasks were under my direct control. Simply, if I wanted to secure an "A" in Entomology, all I had to do was work hard to make it happen. I severely critiqued myself daily. "What could I have done better?" "Why did I think myopically on a particularly abstract issue?" "Did I treat everyone with respect and dignity today?" I was very hard on myself daily by design.

In the Army my concern was to do all the day-to-day activities as well as I could. I never concerned myself about the aggregate view of my achievements; that part of the evaluation process was the Army's job. I was never one to dream about achieving great things. From my very first day in the Army I never coveted promotion. Of course, I wanted to be advanced, but doing my best every day was a far more dominant emotion. I lived the Army's old recruiting slogan to "Be all you can be." Perhaps I just trusted the system and expected that the Army would promote the best officers who possessed the skills it needed. When one's skills were outside the Army's requirements, the next promotion would not be forthcoming. No malice, no shame, it was just good business.

My *aspiration* for thirty-three years in the Army was to give it my best every day. Notably, I *expected* to do my best each day because I worked at it with diligence. The feeling of satisfaction I felt as I left work each day was like a shot of adrenalin. I didn't have to wait for a promotion board to tell me I was doing well. I had critically confirmed my status before I arrived home.

When selections for lieutenant colonel were underway one year, a very good officer came to me and said, "Sir, this promotion is a very important thing in my life. If I don't make lieutenant colonel, I will feel like a failure. Just waiting for the promotion board to announce its findings is driving me crazy. My wife told me I should speak with you and perhaps, I would feel better." We sat for a while and reasoned together as to the probable outcome since I was familiar with his record. Because the promotion selection process was out of his control, he was creating demons, considering all that could go wrong denying him his highly valued promotion. Assuring him of his value to the Army and to the Republic, he left feeling a little better, but until the results of the selection board were announced, he placed himself under needless anxiety by dwelling on the negative outcome of a low probability event, that is, his non-selection for promotion. Of course, he was selected and he reverted back to his cheerful, effective officership. However, for six months he was trapped by his dreams and his dreams were killing him.

Making the choice to develop and take control of your aspirations and expectations is an important step to reduce stress and anxiety while increasing satisfaction and happiness in your life. Such control provides a focus for your zeal and talent. Choose to aspire to the highest standards in your work and your personal life. Then work with dedication every day, expecting to actually achieve those elevated standards. If you can do that, your deeds will separate you from your peers. This kind of dedication isn't easy; you will fail from time to time but persistence and determination are paramount.

I cannot stress this second point with more emphasis: Thou shalt not choose to place your aspirations and expectations under the control of others.

Popularity will not get you promoted, having the boss like you will not get you promoted, smiling a lot and being kind will not get you promoted, but being the most productive, focused, dependable and determined person on the team will propel you up the ladder ahead of your contemporaries. Hard work expertly executed and cheerfully conducted will insure your advancement. If you are not certain that you did your very best, then that is when you should begin to worry.

The decision to manage your aspirations and expectations is one of the most important choices you will make in your life. Contentment is yours when you choose to direct your destiny in concert with your personal and professional goals. This management task will challenge your character to the utmost.

CHAPTER SEVENTEEN

YOU MUST TAKE

BOTH CHEMISTRY AND PHYSICS

The Art of Mentorship

Mentoring is the passing of knowledge, wisdom and experience from one person to another. The intent of mentoring is for a person to grow and mature under a leader's attentive care. A close personal relationship between the mentored and the mentor is essential for successful mentorship because there is, to a certain degree, a melding of the two individuals' characters. To mentor and to have been mentored is an extraordinary gift.

In my mid-teens my parents frequently asked what I wanted to do for my life's work. They posed the question gently and without malice, making it clear that there would be no time later on to "find myself" or locate my niche in life. Now was the time to select a path for my career. They had spent time, money and effort preparing me to go out into the world to take advantage of all that America offered, and they wanted to see results.

The bad news is that, while I wanted to focus, I was unaware of the opportunities available to me. Public school guidance counselors directed me to blue collar jobs, advising me to be realistic about my opportunities in life. To them I was just one more "Italian" kid. They advised me to stay in the family business as I would be assured a good living... What more could I ask? Closing that door, I went to the public library and checked out a few books on careers. I went through the books in a very detailed manner listing every profession I thought I would be interested in pursuing. After a fashion I had a reasonable inventory of careers to consider.

My Dad invited John, the neighborhood sage, to sit with us one evening as we culled out the list. Methodically and with great regard for my desires, we determined that teaching was to be my life's work. My parents were visibly pleased that I had made a wise decision. Just to ensure that I would not change my mind, my career choice was chipped into stone and announced to one and all over the next few days.

A few days later Dad casually asked since I was to be a teacher, what subject would I like to teach. I replied, "A history teacher." He had some concern about that choice and asked, "Do you think you will be able to get a job with a history degree?" I told him the schools were full of history teachers and a job should not be a problem.

My father's mentoring style was Socratic: He asked question after question until I finally arrived at the truth. His next question was, "Where do you want to go to college?" A few years earlier we had agreed that I would pay for my tuition and he would pay for room and board and provide modest spending money. I had worked in the family business since I was ten years old and my father paid me a fair wage. I had a healthy bank account when I was sixteen years old. Although I was very frugal, financing my education quickly became the critical path determining where I would go to college.

My father had a customer who was a high school teacher and a respected man in the community. While speaking with the teacher, Dad asked him to recommend a college that would prepare me for a teaching career. The teacher told my Dad that Indiana State Teachers College (ISTC), just thirty miles down the road, was the perfect place for me to enroll, as ISTC was the best teachers college in Pennsylvania.

The kind man provided my father with application forms and even helped us fill them out. My dad took me to the college in June after my junior year in high school to look the place over and hand carry the application forms and transcripts of my grades to the Admissions Office. In short order I received a letter to report to ISTC to be administered an examination for early acceptance. Since no one in my family knew anything about entrance exams, a quick call to the teacher cleared up the matter. He gave me some ideas how to prepare for the tests. His advice was well received; I did some extra work in math and English and felt comfortable about taking the exams.

On the appointed day in September, I went with my father to ISTC and took the examinations. I also had an interview with the Chairman of the History Department. My dad was present during the interview. After a cordial chat, the professor said that early admission notices for the "Class of 1960" would be dispatched in about a month. My father asked for a few private words with the professor. When that concluded, we drove home feeling really good about ourselves. It was almost as if we had broken a code. We were in the system and hadn't made a mistake.

One evening in October, as we sat for dinner, I found a letter beside my place setting. It was for me from ISTC. Mom told me to wait and open it in front of my father. We sat for dinner, the grace was said, and Dad asked about the letter. I told him the letter was from ISTC and that it was probably my acceptance or rejection letter. Sharply he said, "Open the envelope and don't be so negative."

What he didn't know was that two of my "American" friends at school, who had taken the ISTC entrance exam with me, received their letters of rejection the day before. I assumed that if the college wasn't accepting "Americans," they were surely not going to accept an "Italian." I read the letter aloud. My heart was pumping and blood was rushing to my head. When I heard myself say that I had been accepted for admission to ISTC, I nearly fainted.

I still cannot properly express my joy at being accepted at ISTC. My parents were delighted. My mother in a fit of unregulated pride left the table to telephone my grandparents the good news. Dinner was getting cold and no one seemed to mind.

My grandfather was the only serious person I encountered. He said with some concern that it was now my responsibility to set the example for my brothers, sister and cousins. If I did well in college, they would do well; if I failed, they would most likely avoid following my path for fear of failure. "Unfortunately," he said, "life is like that." Not one to mince words, he placed the monkey squarely on my back. I did everything I could to make money for my college fund in my high school senior year. I did not participate in many school activities. Still, I had my friends and my bank account was growing nicely.

My father was my first and most important mentor in my life. He asked the right questions about my future and kept asking them until he got the proper answer. He actually made me feel as if I were forging my own path. When my reasoning on an issue was skewed, he went back into the Socratic mode until I sorted it out. I occasionally challenged his virtues but I did not rebel. By my father's example and instruction I learned the value and management of money.

His lessons on interpersonal relationships and communication techniques with customers were a valuable lifetime gift. My Dad's sense of humor was something to emulate. He fostered my spiritual development; confident spirituality proved to be a steadying force in my turbulent life. He would not tolerate lying, cheating or stealing. Observing his sensitivity to the needs of others made me a more compassionate person.

Of notable importance, he also taught me the wonderful game of golf. The life lessons learned under my father's tutelage were precious gifts. I was prepared to manage the good and bad of life's experiences when I left his care. He repeatedly said, "You know what must be done. Go do it."

I met my second mentor during freshman orientation at ISTC. Having found the registration lines for history majors long and disorderly, I wandered into the gym to look around. I noticed that it had also been set up to accept students to register for classes. In contrast to the auditorium where the history students were engaged in hand-to-hand combat for classes, this place was almost empty. A middle-aged man with a flower in his lapel was reading a newspaper with his feet propped up on a table. Looking over the newspaper, he said, "Can I help you, son?" I walked over and told him of my intent to look over the gym and we struck up a conversation.

He asked what I planned to study. I told the story about being accepted to study history and the bedlam at the auditorium. The conversation was pleasant, the man seemed friendly and I liked him. When I asked him what he taught, he told me he was a biology professor. We talked a bit about the sciences and the course of study for a degree. Then it just came out of my mouth: "Is it possible to transfer from history to biology?" He said that it was easily done but wanted to know why I wanted to transfer. I told him truthfully that I had done well in biology, chemistry, and physics in high school and that I liked him. If he would be my advisor, I wanted to transfer as a biology major. "Before we take this too far," he said, "you must understand that I will insist that you take both chemistry and physics as a minor." No problem, I could do that.

That was it, the deal was done. He signed me up in a flash, and I was out of there as a biology major. No dreams of greatness, no life goals, no intention for a career in science, I wasn't even wild about taking chemistry and physics. The truth was that I liked the man. He was honest; he clearly communicated that he would hold me to a high standard; he would responsibly dictate my course of study; and above all, he would require that I apply myself to the utmost of my ability. That evening as I was assessing the events of the day, I thought about what I had done.

Without a doubt or a negative thought, I decided that, since I really didn't know anything about this college business, I needed a person who cared about my intellectual, psychological, and physical well-being for the next four years. It really did not matter what I studied. The important thing was that I had to grow and mature in many ways. If I was to be like someone when I grew up, I wanted to be like Dr. Willis Bell.

Over the next four years there were moments when I regretted my decision to pursue an undergraduate degree under his tutelage. It turns out that he was too much like my dad. He signed me up for the toughest courses; he accepted no excuses; and he insisted on the highest standards in my work. He challenged me in every way possible. On the other hand, when he heard of my deal with my father that I would pay my tuition, he hired me as an assistant and paid me $30 per month for my work supporting his laboratory classes. He was more than generous and really cared for me. At Christmas he always gave me a gift of a few dollars.

Dr. Bell was my guiding light at ISTC; I grew under his care. He was my trusted friend and my mentor. He instilled academic discipline, reinforced my persistence and determination to excel and compassionately cared for my personal welfare. Attendance at college was not just an accumulation of credits and taking mandatory courses for me. I had all of that, of course, but I had to satisfy Dr. Bell that my motivation for studying was to achieve excellence in my work. There was no card punching for that man.

Dr. Bell reinforced my father's virtues and added to my character development. He taught me how to work under pressure without stress. Notably, Dr. Bell kept me in overload and under pressure for three years. I emerged from his tutelage capable of skillfully accomplishing difficult tasks, under a variety of stresses, cheerfully and with enthusiasm. He also gave me the gift of knowing when to employ detailed technical analysis and when abstract perspectives were appropriate. Dr. Bell's greatest gift of mentorship was instilling intellectual toughness and the capability to maintain a cool head when others were faltering under real or imagined pressures.

We had hard words on only one occasion and that was in the last semester of my senior year. He successfully had arranged a fully funded master's degree program for me at a nearby college. I had spoken seriously to him about going into the Army for a few years as I had been designated an ROTC Distinguished Military Graduate. The Army sounded interesting to me. He said, "Forget the commission. If you get drafted, tell them what you have studied. You will be out in two years." The moment arrived when I could no longer delay the Army/Master's Degree decision. I told Dr. Bell the evening before I signed that I had made the choice to try the Army. I assured him I would stay for only three years and would be back. He took me firmly by the arm, looked me dead in the eye and with a pained look on his face said, "If you stay in the Army for three years, they will keep you for a lifetime." Dr. Bell understood the Army and me better than I did. The Army did get a hold on me and I did stay for a long time.

The third important mentor in my life was Colonel William D. Beard. He was the commander of the Division Support Command in the 8th Infantry Division. He selected me to work on his staff when I was a young captain. He was a highly decorated war hero and a man of extraordinary strength of character. I was intent on leaving the Army until I met him. Colonel Beard was my first and most important Army role model.

He gave me many professional opportunities to grow and I enjoyed the challenges. He worked with me to ensure that I never went astray but he always allowed me to take the lead in achieving the goal he set for me. Colonel Beard had a calmness in critical situations that I envied. He was always a gentleman, but if you crossed his path, you would wish that you hadn't. He was a bulldog in problem solving and a man who always told the full and complete truth. To have the opportunity to serve with a man like that day in and day out was a privilege. He set the standard for my military service.

Colonel Beard was an excellent writer. Over the years when I believed that I required his wisdom, I would write him a letter stating the issue at hand. He would respond with his thoughts on the matter. I saved those letters and, from time to time, I reread some of my favorites. I still marvel at the clarity of his insight.

Colonel Beard regularly exposed me to generals and colonels. I developed an understanding of their responsibilities and was not awed by the symbols of their rank. By his example I learned to speak to powerful men with clarity, tact and absolute veracity. Because of his command responsibilities, Colonel Beard was frequently compelled to make and execute difficult decisions. I was a firsthand witness to his technique in managing these sensitive matters. He ensured the tasks were performed swiftly, efficiently and with dignity for all concerned. Watching him perform on a daily basis, he gained my utmost respect. My common sense compelled me to emulate his personality and professional practices.

Colonel Beard told me that "if I stayed out of trouble," I would be a general officer one day. He wrote that comment on my performance report when I had only six years in the Army. As much as I emulated my father and Dr. Bell I was now also patterning my behavior in the Colonel Bill Beard mode. It was a prudent choice.

My father could not guide me at college or in the Army as he did at home. Dad met Dr. Bell on a few occasions and I believe he willingly passed me off to his care while I was in college. Though he never met Colonel Beard, I believe he would have approved of his mentoring style as well. These three men were remarkably alike. They were strong of character, held high standards and would accept nothing less from me. My intellect and personality are in large part a collage of these three men. They all had the same agenda...they were going to help me be all I could be.

People are not mentored when they hitch their wagon to the boss and merely follow him up the corporate ladder. Mentoring occurs when a person grows and matures personally and professionally under a leader's attentive care. The value of enlightened mentorship cannot be overstated. Mentoring is passing the wisdom of the elders in a very personal and almost private fashion. It is an art form and must be practiced.

Mentoring is not easy or pleasant. Challenging people to standards higher than their peers requires sensitive attention, persistence, and determination on the part of both the mentor and the mentored. The rewards are marvelous and failures are deep wounds because mentors relinquish a part of their soul to the mentored.

Mentorship is not favoritism. To be mentored skillfully and attentively is a gift...it is a gift to be shared. Those who have been mentored must not fail to share this special wisdom.

Some years ago I was selected to lecture at the Army Command and General Staff College and provide my thoughts on the importance of mentorship. Recorded below are my notes for those sessions:

1. Mentors are first and foremost teachers.
2. Mentors are focused and strong of character. They are also patient and understanding.
3. Mentors are trusted friends. Their friendship is a shield.
4. Mentors are talented communicators.
5. Mentors have a sense of humor. To laugh together is a gift.
6. Mentors are not jealous or selfish.
7. Mentors insure that ethics rule the conduct of business.
8. Mentors are motivators enticing the mentored to take on difficult jobs cheerfully.
9. Mentors take the time to seriously address the thoughts of the mentored.
10. Mentors look for the mentored to demonstrate a moral potential.

These ten thoughts are the common product of the three men in my life who helped me to never shirk my duties and always give every task, no matter how small, my best effort. Make the choice to mentor and, if mentorship is offered, make the choice to accept it. Your personality will be favorably shaped and your performance will be enhanced in the process. Engaging in the process of mentorship is a choice well made. The relationship will last a lifetime. I promise you will never be the same... You will only be better.

CHAPTER EIGHTEEN

YOU CAN'T HAVE EVERYTHING

Perspectives on the Marital Relationship

Marriage has been studied and analyzed in detail. Such efforts, for the most part, reflect marriage as a complex association of two individuals with innate, gender-divergent perspectives of life. On the other hand, for many of us marriage is a simple relationship based on trust and love with many options for men and women to happily accommodate each other's needs and goals. Keep it simple, trust in and care for each other and married life will be a joyous affair.

When I was nineteen years old I was an altar boy at St. Therese Catholic Church in Johnstown, Pennsylvania. I regularly served the 11:30 a.m. Mass each Sunday in the summer while home from college.

One Sunday in early May, Anita Sabo came to communion at the 11:30 Mass and she caught my eye. I knew her family well, and being two years younger than I, she was a classmate of my brother Sam. I remembered Anita as a cute, petite girl who was bright, enthusiastic and wore her hair in a ponytail. Having been away at college, I hadn't seen Anita for two years and was amazed at the difference two years could make. She was lovely and delightfully curvy. After Mass I had dinner with my family and then called Anita for a date. After checking with her parents, she accepted. From that moment on, I was captured.

I was immediately attracted to her because she was cute, intelligent and filled with prudent enthusiasm. She was not shy about candidly speaking her mind but was also sweet, kind and thoughtful. Anita was so naïve and trusting that I just wanted to keep her safe from anything harsh. We shared a common life goal to do our best as God gave us the light to see it. There was no competition between us; we grew together complementing each other. Just being with her made me happy. All things considered, I suspect that if you are an altar boy eyeing the girls coming to communion, you are probably too old to be an altar boy. On the other hand, it is not a bad thing to discover the woman of your life in a church.

Anita had just graduated from Johnstown High School and was to attend Indiana State Teachers College in the fall. I was thrilled that we would be going to college together. The Sabo family lived just up the hill from our home and I spent many evenings that summer on her front porch. Actually, it was Anita, her father and me. I had known Joe Sabo since I was a boy and having him sit with us was not an issue. We talked easily together. Our families operated from the same baseline of virtues, attitudes and standards. Anita's dad and my father were very good friends. When my father was courting my mother, Anita's dad gave my dad flowers from the Sabo family greenhouse to help him impress my mother. My dear father-in-law would frequently joke, noting, "If it weren't for me, you might not be here."

In October, I gave Anita my fraternity pin. I had been struck by the Sicilian love thunderbolt and for me this was more than an adolescent statement of affection. The pin was a commitment of marriage in lieu of an engagement ring. Simply put, I did not have the money to purchase a proper ring. She was so dear to me that the conventional symbol of my commitment would have to wait until I could do it properly. My father was thrilled that I was attracted to a bright, strong-willed but loving young woman who was the daughter of a good friend. He hoped she would be able to control my stubbornness and help focus my enthusiasm. My mother was certain that Anita had the "right stuff" to "handle" me. Given that Anita was a religious and spiritual woman, Mom felt that Anita would be able to tolerate me for the long term. Prayer, according to my mother, was an essential element in this regard.

Anita's parents were happy with me. My persistence and determination were considered to be positive character traits for a successful career. Besides, her father really liked me and I really liked him. Both sets of parents asked, and we promised, that we would not marry until we both graduated from college. Anita and I kept that promise.

That October my father said it would be a respectful act on my part if I asked my grandparents for their blessing on our proposed marriage. He assured me that the act was more an Italian culture event than American but that there would be wisdom in their thoughts and I would be better for the experience. Of course I agreed, as I loved my grandparents very much.

A few days later my mother called me at the college to advise that I would meet with Grandfather Coco the coming Friday evening to ask his blessing. I was asked to wear a white shirt, tie, and sport coat for the occasion. Sicilian respect for another person was often demonstrated by one's manner of dress and courtesy when they met. To appear in casual dress would be an indication that I was something less than serious about the meeting. To be prepared, I asked my parents what to say and what to expect when I spoke with my grandfather.

Surprisingly, they pulled a Pontius Pilate and washed their hands of the matter. Dad gave me the car and I was off into the unknown, flying solo.

I arrived at my grandparents' home in the early evening. My grandfather was sitting on the front porch. When he saw me, he seemed surprised and said, "Joey, I am so happy, why have you come to see me?"

My first thought was that this was supposed to be all arranged, so why the surprise? My second thought was that this was probably some time-honored Sicilian introduction to the blessing process. Temporarily losing control of the mind-mouth linkage, I heard myself say, "I have come to ask your blessing to be married." I hadn't even said "Hello." I had bounded over the salutations and blurted out my mission.

My grandfather was a smooth operator. He invited me to sit. By his manner he communicated that he was in charge and that I was to listen. He said, "I am pleased that you have come to ask my blessing in marriage. Before I give that blessing, I want to ask some questions and pass on a few words of wisdom." Relieved that he was in the "transmit" mode and I was in "receive," I began to relax a little.

His first question was, "Do you love Anita?" I told him I loved her so much that I couldn't think of life without her. He noted that if I had said anything less, he would have been reluctant to give his blessing. He then advised me that once this commitment was made there would be no other woman in my life, ever. "You have seen me, your father, and your uncles; we are men faithful to our wives, and I expect that you will be the same. To fail in this is to jeopardize your relationship with your wife. Women are

very sensitive to infidelity and in this matter you cannot fail."
I assured him that his words were well received.

Then he said, "You must be 'the Big Umbrella.' Your wife must always feel happy and secure under the protection of your umbrella. She should want for nothing within reason. Accordingly, you should be kind and understand that she looks at the world much differently than you. She will get excited over issues that defy logic. She will worry needlessly over issues of little consequence. You will never quite understand why she is happy or why she is sad. Comfort her when she is in need. Try to understand her the best you can. Don't be too stubborn and only draw the line in the sand when it is absolutely necessary. If you must have an argument, be certain it is a significant issue. Avoid conflict over small things.

"Anita will remember every argument you ever had and will remind you of them when it is most uncomfortable for you. Her life will be made pleasant if you compliment her on her accomplishments and her appearance. Sometimes just a tender touch will say more than one hundred words. Your wife and your children will have a good life under your Big Umbrella and you will be loved and respected. You have seen your father, your uncles, and me; follow our example." There were no conditionals in his lecture. Finally he said, "If you do this well, your life will be enriched by her love. You must be the Big Umbrella." When he finished he asked, firmly, "Do you understand?"

I told him that I understood completely and that I was anxiously looking forward to my investiture as the Big Umbrella. That was the A+ answer. He then asked me if I wanted some coffee. We retired to the kitchen where he poured two strong Italian coffees. We carried them to the porch and talked about college and life in general. Man-to-man stuff. When the coffee was gone he said, "You have my blessing, but remember you must be the Big Umbrella." He was very deliberate every time he used that phrase and said it so often that it could not be forgotten. We kissed and, while driving home, the Big Umbrella was all I could think about. Notably, my grandmother was nowhere to be seen during this entire adventure. I suspected that was probably due to some long-standing unwritten Rule for the Blessing.

My parents were on the swing on the back porch when I arrived. They were eager to know the contents of my conversation with my grandfather. I said, "He asked me if I loved Anita and then he told me that I must be The Big Umbrella." My father was pleased with this summary and asked if I fully understood my grandfather's wisdom. When I assured him that I had gotten it all, the matter seemed closed. My mother was not so easily satisfied; she wanted more detail. I felt uncomfortable discussing the manly secrets of wife management that my grandfather had just passed on to me so I remained abstract about the conversation. I thought, perhaps, it was some sort of confidential masculine tract that had been revealed to me. I was not about to spill the beans. When she asked me how long the conversation lasted, I told her, "Maybe ten minutes, then we had some coffee."

Briskly, she announced "Next week you will speak with your grandmother." I looked at my dad and he just shrugged his shoulders. He wasn't prepared to draw any lines in the sand on this issue. I was still on the hot seat.

My grandmother was a strong, kind, and loving woman. She was the only person I ever saw confront my grandfather. The issue was never an important one but she would show her disgust with his stubbornness by turning her back, walking away, and saying the word in the Sicilian dialect for "jack-ass" just loud enough for him to hear it. I never knew him to respond; he got the message, loud and clear.

When my mother called me at college the next week, she told me that I was to meet with my grandmother on Friday evening. At the appointed hour on Friday, and now being an experienced Blessing Requestor, I dressed appropriately, asked for no additional instructions, jumped into Dad's car and headed for my grandparents' home.

I knocked at the front door and entered. Grandmother was sitting in the parlor on a Florentine chair by the desk. My grandfather had been nattily dressed the week before, but my grandmother even more so; her hair was styled and she was dressed, complete with pearls. I quickly received the signal: This session was important. My grandfather was nowhere in sight. Predictably, she said, "Joey, it is so nice that you should visit. Why have you come to see me?"

I replied confidently, "Nana, I have come to ask for your blessing to be married." She gently asked me to be seated and pointed to an ottoman stool adjacent to her chair. On a good day Nana was five feet tall. When I sat on the ottoman, I found that she was sitting higher than I and that I was looking up at her. No man-to-man stuff here. I was uncomfortable, suspecting that I had been put in a defensive position.

I was stunned when she asked, "What is the name of the woman you intend to marry?" Knowing that no question from a Sicilian is ever loosely presented, my mind reeled at the query, but in a nanosecond I realized that this must be one of those blessing format questions.

I answered in an assured voice, "Nana, it is Anita."

She answered, "Anita is a wonderful girl. She is loving, bright and strong; she will make you a fine home and give you good children." Then she said, "Before I give my blessing I have a few questions." She was following my grandfather's story line but I was a little tense. When she asked, "Do you love her with your heart and soul?" I responded, as before, that I could not imagine life without her; a truthful answer that hit the jackpot the week before. My grandmother calmly replied that my love and fidelity to Anita were imperative and that was good. Last week, this was the keystone question; today it was a lead in to something larger.

"Now the second question," She said as she raised her right hand from her lap and, with her index finger, pointing skyward asked, "Is Anita a Catholic?"

My mind began to tumble. We had attended Mass together, taken communion; Anita's credentials in this matter were beyond question. Was I being set up for something that would deny me her blessing? Once again, losing the brain-to-mouth connection, I heard myself saying, "Yes, Nana, she is a Catholic."

My grandmother replied softly that it was very important for the wife to be a practicing Catholic as she would set the religious standards for the family. I would most likely be too busy with my work and, not having time to participate, would pass this important matter in her direction. She told me to listen to Anita's advice on matters of religion. My very salvation was at stake.

Where was she was going with this line of discussion? Nana had taught me to say the "Our Father" and the "Hail Mary" prayers in Italian as well as English. When I visited her alone, before I could leave to go home, we would say these prayers together in both languages. How could she say that I would be preoccupied and not pay attention to religion? My grandfather's words came to me in a flash: "Try to understand a woman as best you can." My best course of action was to be cool, continue to answer truthfully and let the chips fall where they may. I knew that I was going under, but unfortunately, I didn't know when or how deep I would sink.

Nana, raising that index finger to the heavens again, said, "Now, the last question...Joey, is she an Italian?" That was the torpedo that hit below my intellectual waterline. Almost everyone knows that Sabo (Anglicized from Szabo) is a Hungarian name. No one ever told me that I was required to marry an Italian girl. Was this grounds for withholding a blessing?

Almost defiantly I answered, "No, Nana, she is not Italian." My grandmother then pointed her finger directly at me, and in her kind, but firm voice said, "Joey, that is your first lesson about marriage... YOU CAN'T HAVE EVERYTHING!" There it was: Checkmate. I had nothing to say.

Her manner quickly became almost playful as she explained my need to understand, compromise and to accommodate my wife's feminine nature. She advised that married life was a series of ups and downs and that it was how I handled the "downs" that mattered. She advised me that I had many of my grandfather's personality traits. "Being stubborn like a donkey will not serve you well," she advised. "Talk to your wife; listen to her concerns and ask her point of view on issues that affect the family. Do this and I promise that the downs will not be so deep and they will be short lived."

My grandmother assured me that I would be prosperous in life's work and that I would be a good provider as that was "in my blood." She was quick to add that it was also in my blood not to be completely sensitive to the feelings of others. "Anita," she said, "has enough feelings for the both of you. Listen to her and heed her counsel."

"When there is a problem with the children, listen to her advice," she said. "Do not act imprudently by yourself. When you do act, be certain that both of you agree as to how the matter should be handled. She will teach the children character and you must be the example for them to follow."

"Anita will see and feel more than you and will keep many things unsaid in her heart. That is a woman's way. You can make her life happy by being thoughtful and generous. Nothing extravagant is necessary; a small gift, occasionally, as a symbol of your affection is important. Compliment her on her appearance, take her out to dinner, make her feel special and you will be a king in your own home."

Nana made it clear that Anita would see me as her partner and the most important person in her life. As such, I was to reassure her of the importance of her work in our home. "Anyone can get a job in town; that is easy work," she said. "But it takes a strong, smart woman to make and maintain a happy home, manage her children, support her husband and enjoy her friends." She told me she was assured of my love for and gentle kindness toward Anita.

Then she told me that it was also in my blood to think that whatever I had - wife, children or house - was the best in the world, even if they weren't. That was nature; men were like that. She said that Anita would see things as they are; that was a woman's nature. If braggadocio was a male fault, worry and concern were the woman's. If we dealt with the major issues in life together, nature would balance things out properly and we would prosper.

Nana made a clear point that we were to grow together. She made reference to a couple I knew where the man grew professionally and socially while his wife remained a thirty-year-old woman with the social skills of a teenage girl. It was my responsibility to give my wife opportunities and encourage her to grow along with me. "Further," she said, "Anita will have some activities that may not interest you, but you owe it to her to learn to like the opera, to shop without complaint, or to enjoy and respect her friends as you would your own."

We spoke at some length about my domestic skill shortfalls and my inherited personality defects. She ended every criticism of my personality with, "But you have been given the gift of a good intellect, you are a determined young man; you will be a good protector and provider for your family."

Clearly, Nana was getting tired as we had been talking for nearly an hour. She looked in my eyes and took my hand and said, "You have been blessed with a good family. You have selected a good woman for your wife and only opportunity awaits both of you. You think that you cannot love her more than you do now. In a few years, after good times and some hard times together, you will look back and realize that it was only the beginning of your affection. I wish for you the love and comfort that your grandfather and I have known together. You have my blessing, I am confident in your happiness together." She left me with these parting words, "Remember, don't be stubborn like a donkey."

We kissed and I hugged her not really understanding everything she said but remembering it all for the time when I could better understand. When I returned home, my mother had already spoken with my grandmother which relieved me of the requirement to debrief. My parents were satisfied that I had been passed the Wisdom of My Elders. The rest was up to me.

I had another very special conversation with my grandfather about married life shortly after my grandmother died. Burned into my soul are his last thoughts and words that evening. He told me of his deep love for my grandmother and the joy of their life together. He spoke of some of their cherished moments together, their love for their children and grandchildren; he never said a negative word.

As he was finishing, he said that Nana loved him so much that he was in her last thoughts even as she was dying; that her last words were softly calling his name. There was a long pause, and then he said, "She is with God." He could not continue and began to weep, sobbing quietly, and in the darkness of the room I quickly joined him. That was the last time I was alone with my grandfather. Mike Coco, a healthy man, died suddenly the next month. It did not require a doctor to ascertain the cause of his passing.

There is no defined equation for a happy marriage. Because of our work, personalities, and personal goals, there are thousands of variables to be managed.

However, there are at least three immutable factors in the marital relationship of a man and a woman. They are mutual love, respect, and unquestioned fidelity to each other.

Once these elements are in place, the variables can be managed to fit the couple. Naturally there will be conflicts in the relationship; that is normal. The issue is to resolve them promptly and without resentment held by either party. It takes a while to learn this as it is not easy. Never stop working on this issue as it washes unwanted stress and needless anxiety from your life.

Seek special time together. Those events will be remembered fondly and for a very long time. Speak kind, complimentary and loving words sincerely to each other. Often they are the adhesive that bonds the bricks of love, respect and fidelity tightly together. Keep a sense of humor. A good laugh is often better than two Tylenol.

The differences between men and women are not antagonistic, as some would propose. Rather, they are complementary and reinforcing. It is an act of nature. There are many ways to find joy and peace in marriage. Firmly establish the immutables and the rest is art form. Above all, remember: YOU CAN'T HAVE EVERYTHING!!!

CHAPTER NINETEEN

UNCLE DOMINIC

Verifiable Information is Paramount

There are usually two reasons why verifiable information is unavailable to decision makers. First, adversaries may conceal the truth and make false information available to flaw your decision making process. More often, analysis, errors, assumptions, poor information collection and incomplete but rapid communication of a situation may misrepresent the complete truth. Secure timely, credible information to minimize the potential for embarrassment or failure.

In an information rich culture, individuals are required to make judgments every day concerning the completeness and quality of information received. The choices made after processing that information often determine important issues in our personal and professional lives. Verifiable information produces mostly positive choices while biased, incomplete or misrepresented data will guarantee a choice destined to some form of failure.

I have used the Uncle Dominic story as a lighthearted and effective introduction to many of my lectures. My intent was to illustrate that even well-intentioned people can unintentionally communicate information that can be misinterpreted. The punch line to the story is that, if you question the information you are receiving, you are compelled to challenge it to arrive at the truth. Further, the person passing the information has the responsibility to pass information with absolute clarity. The Uncle Dominic story goes like this:

There was to be a large family affair in Johnstown and the invitation to attend was an offer one could not refuse. Living near Richmond, Virginia, we packed up the boys and the dog and headed off for western Pennsylvania, arriving late at night. My mother was excited about the affair as she would see some cousins that she had not seen in some time. I was less excited about the whole event. Dear Anita, ever dutiful to these matters, polished up the boys for the extended reception and dinner.

Arriving at the door of the hotel ballroom, we made it a point to say hello and kiss and hug everyone in sight. I had not lived in my hometown for some time. Many of my relatives had matured and frankly, their looks had changed to the point where I could not identify some of them. When an elderly woman cheerily asked, "Do you remember me?" I had to confess that a lot of water had passed beneath my bridge (that is Johnstown Flood talk for "I don't know") and would appreciate it if she could help me a bit. After a few clues I remembered her name; she was so pleased. At that point, it never dawned on me that someone might not remember exactly who I was. Passing through the receiving line, I entered the ballroom.

Across the room I saw Uncle Dominic. He was a nice man in his 80's. When he looked in my direction and smiled, I headed towards him. He was surrounded by some young women and a sixty- something woman who was on his arm.

She laughed every time he spoke. The ladies were fussing over him and he was the center of their attention.

Approaching, I noticed he was wearing a Milan cut, double-breasted, dark blue suit that fit perfectly. His shirt was brilliant white and he was wearing a Como silk tie. His silver hair was razor cut. Uncle Dominic was a handsome old gentleman.

Now, I must advise that my youngest brother Michael, a medical doctor, has a facial resemblance to me; we are the same height, the same weight and his voice sounds similar to mine.

Joining the covey of women surrounding Uncle Dominic, I did not identify myself but cheerfully greeted everyone like a politician running for office. When I stood in front of Uncle Dominic I said to him, "It is so nice to see you again. I love your suit, the tie is super...you look like a million bucks."

He extended his hand smiling and was looking deeply into my face. We shook hands and I said, "Uncle Dominic, your handshake is strong, you have good color in your face, and your hand is so steady it could be the hand of a surgeon. I should be so healthy when I am your age."

Releasing my hand he became very serious, delayed speaking for just a moment and said slowly, almost in a *Godfather* movie- type voice, "I am getting to be an old man and sometimes my eyes don't work so good. Tell me...are you the doctor or are you the soldier?" The group went silent and all eyes turned to me awaiting my answer. Not wanting to lose my momentum, with pride in my voice I confidently said, "Uncle Dominic, I am Joe, the soldier."

With that he stood erect, pointed the mandatory index finger skyward and said with loud authority, "In that case, Mr. Soldier, your opinions on the condition of my health don't count!"

When he said the word "count," he thrust that finger into the air above his head. There was a bellow of laughter from the ladies surrounding us which carried across the ball-room. Wanting to keep my embarrassment to a minimum, Uncle Dominic took my face in his hands and kissed my cheeks. While the women were still laughing, he whispered, "Don't be upset; at my age I must quickly separate the sheep from the goats. I know you meant well, but I was looking for a medical opinion. It is important to know who you are speaking to when addressing such matters." I have not taken the liberty to comment on someone's apparent health ever since.

While I assuredly, but unintentionally, misrepresented myself to Uncle Dominic, ascertaining the credibility of an information source was a point well made. Then in the lecture introduction I would note that while I did not know the difference between halitosis and diverticulitis, I did have some serious insights into the business of logistics. With that, I proceeded with the business of the lecture. To this day, people still will ask me how dear old Uncle Dominic is doing. While he has gone to his eternal reward, his legacy lives on.

Just as Uncle Dominic's source vetting process clarified the issue, the same process will assist you in separating the informational sheep from the goats. Usually in professional and personal affairs the source validation process takes time and effort. It is not always easy. Make the choice to ask questions and place all the facts on the table at the outset of your decision-making. This will minimize anxiety and embarrassment later. When the facts bearing on the problem change midstream, because of a failure to validate them early on, issue resolution is more difficult.

Many failings in the management process are the result of erroneous assumptions at the outset of analysis. Make the choice to seriously question critical information. There are usually a few snakes under the rocks when you get into the details.

Make the choice to ensure that flawed information is not resident in your decisions. If information is less than fact-based, be certain that it is clearly noted, documented and seek more definition of the data. Life will be a lot more pleasant, better decisions will result and outcomes will have a greater probability for success once you "separate the sheep from the goats."

CHAPTER TWENTY

WALKING THE DOG

Success and Responsibility

Making the choice to develop and achieve a moral and ethical character leads to personal success. Strength of character manifests itself in elevated performance in the execution of one's duties and responsibilities. Performance marked by honors and awards rests on a foundation of credible character. To be both successful in character and responsible in duty is the goal.

My father was never enamored of my choice of the Army as a career. On the day I was commissioned, my parents held a party in our home and I wore my uniform. When the celebration ended, my father got me off to the side and said, "You are my son and you are very important to me. I have no affection for the Army and I am asking, from this day forward, that you never wear the Army uniform in my home. In fact, I hope never to see you wear that uniform again."

"You are always welcome in our home, but you will wear civilian clothes here," he continued in a warm and friendly tone. There was no malice in his words; he was simply stating his preference.

Knowing that he must have his reasons, I assured him he would not see the uniform again. I kissed him, we shook hands and I went to pack for my departure. My father saw me in a uniform only once during the next twenty years. I honored his wish. While he would speak in prideful terms of my brothers' and sister's professional careers he never expressed an interest in my professional life and would say, "And Joe is in the Army."

Fast-forwarding to January 1981, I had been selected for promotion to colonel the previous summer and had also been selected to command the 8th Support Group in Livorno, Italy. I am uncertain of my motives but I felt that after twenty years it was time for me to solicit my father's acknowledgment that I was doing well in my life's work. I hoped to excite his pride by advising him I was to be a colonel and command a large organization in Italy. Perhaps I could even entice him to visit us in "the old country." Anita had arranged for my parents to visit our home in Springfield, Virginia prior to our leaving for Italy; the iron was hot.

My folks arrived on a Saturday. We had a wonderful time all day. We never spoke of the Army or the impending move to Italy. On Sunday after Holy Mass we had a large dinner. About three o'clock my father said to me, "Why don't we take a walk?" Heather, our dog, a wirehaired fox terrier, was unaware that she was a dog. She thought she was our fourth child. When she heard the word "walk" she ran for the leash by the door, picked it up with her teeth and carried it to my dad. My father had no particular affection for animals, but he thought Heather was cute and smart so he said, "Let's take the dog."

The day was cold and windy and we were wearing overcoats, gloves and hats. The dog was thrilled to accompany us and we departed for a walk around the block. Dad was getting up in years and did not want to fall, so he held the dog's leash in one hand and my arm with the other. After some small talk, I decided this was the proper time to solicit some recognition and approval for my accomplishments over the past twenty years. We were just passing out to the main street when I advised him that we would be moving to Italy in a few months. His reply was abrupt, noting that my mother told him of our departure. His tone of voice was a sign to back off; he was uncomfortable talking about the Army.

I was determined to discuss this issue with my father so I continued. I told him it was an honor to be advanced to the rank of colonel. Further, to be selected to command at the brigade level was an expression of the Army's belief in my potential for continued advancement. The Old Boy remained silent, walking briskly and looking straight ahead. I then said, "Dad. I have done very well in the Army. I have been successful in my profession." The word "successful" didn't get out of my mouth when he stopped dead in his tracks. Letting loose of my arm, he turned me quickly towards him and said firmly, "You think promotion and increased responsibility is success? Let me tell you about success.

"Your mother and I have four children. None of you has ever been in trouble at school or in the community. In fact, all of you have brought honor to your mother and me by your achievements. You have been respectful and loving children. That is success. Secondly, all our children are married and none has suffered the pain of divorce. You have happy homes, you love your children and they love you. All four of you have ensured that your children know and love your mother and me. That is success."

Then he said, "All of our children have a firm belief in the Almighty. The strength that comes from that belief in dealing with the problems of daily life is extraordinary. When you are overwhelmed by problems at home or at work, you have a rock around which you can throw a rope. You will never be swept away by events. We have given that gift of faith to our children and they have accepted it. That is success!"

"Your mother and I worked very hard with each of our children to ensure a positive development of character. That is success!"

"This business of promotion to colonel and being selected for a command, whatever that is, has nothing to do with *success*. It has everything to do with your *responsibilities*." More fired up than ever, he said, "Simply, you go to work, do well, and the Army, whoever that is, decides to give you more work and greater responsibilities."

He finished with a flourish reverting to his time-tested mode of defining the situation in a fable. He continued, "To the Army you are a donkey. They put a pack on your back, fill the pack with rocks, and tell you to run up the hill, dump the rocks, and run back down for another load. You are a strong, smart donkey and you carry more rocks to the top than the other donkeys. When the Army sees that you are better than the other donkeys your age going up and down the mountain, they give you a few younger donkeys to follow your lead to carry more rocks to the top of the hill. Because you care for your younger brother donkeys, you find a shorter, less fatiguing route to the top. You make sure they have hay and water and get some sleep before you allow yourself to eat, drink and sleep. They observe your strength of character and begin to emulate the virtues of your character.

"It does not go unnoticed that you developed a good plan for work and put concern for your brother donkeys before your own welfare. This motivates your younger donkeys to excel and you get recognition from a big donkey for your effort. I have no doubt that if you continue to carry rocks efficiently and sincerely look after the donkeys entrusted to your care, some day you will be a big donkey." I believe that some droplet of Aesop's blood flowed in my father's veins. He was really good at this.

Then in a stern voice he noted, "You will achieve your personal successes and professional responsibilities on the foundation of a moral character. You must always be alert to the health of your character as it alone sustains the quality of your performance as a husband, father and soldier." With that said, he visibly settled down, half-smiled and petted the dog's head. As we moved on, we spoke only of developing the character of my three sons as if nothing had happened. We never spoke of the matter again. I did not feel rebuffed by his response. Actually, I even felt a little better that I had one more story gem to put in my kit bag. He knew my life was going to become more intense and, in his own way, was still helping me focus and prepare.

My father finally caved in to my mother and attended my promotion ceremony to colonel in the Pentagon in late spring. Dad was not comfortable entering the Pentagon and it showed. He was brought into the room where the promotion would take place and he was wearing his "Sicilian Face." It scared the hell out of some of the attendees. There were whispers of Mafia. After the ceremony I was asked if he was a Mafia Don. I advised them that he was not a Mafioso but was a no-nonsense American gentleman of high standards. I also advised them it was foolishness to cross his path. To a man, all believed me.

After the promotion, I served in Italy for three years and was eventually back working in the Pentagon. The job was demanding. My parents visited our home in Alexandria, Virginia in May, 1985. My father died suddenly in June.

The selection list for promotion to brigadier general was to be released in July 1985; I was a candidate for advancement. In early July I left the Pentagon just as it was beginning to get dark and headed home. As one drives south on the George Washington Parkway, past Reagan National Airport, you will drive up a small hill as you are about to enter Old Town Alexandria. There is a stoplight at the top of that hill. I was tired and the light went red just as I approached. I was irritated by the delay but slowed to a stop. As I sat there waiting for the light to change, I heard my father's voice in the car. It was clear and distinct.

The voice said, "Joe, soon you will learn of your selection for promotion to brigadier general. We are proud... You will not fail." I was struck with fear and tears were flowing from my eyes. The light changed and I slowly advanced into Old Town. The event was over as quickly as it started; I was shaken by the experience.

The next day I was told of my selection to brigadier general. Being selected was an honor, but having had the event in Alexandria, the experience was an assurance that my father believed that I had made the right choice to dedicate my life responsibilities to protect and defend our precious Constitution. I slept well believing he was proud that I had sorted out my successes and my responsibilities. I had made the proper choices and felt good.

My father and I were miles apart on the Army as a career. However, that did not mean that we were compelled to reject each other. It was my responsibility to accommodate him on this issue. The directive, as he so often pointed out, was to "Honor your father and your mother." We loved each other and were proud of each other as individuals. In this world, he did not like what I did for my life's work. However, that was a matter of lesser importance. Showing respect and honoring the man for his role as a caring father was the proper choice.

Dad said that professional accomplishments were a result of skillful and attentive execution of one's responsibilities. Raising children to be good citizens, honorable men and women, with a firm belief in the Almighty, all desired, planned, and executed by parents seeking the best from their children, was true success. One could ask no more from life. He believed that family and business were separate issues as were success and responsibility.

To be successful *and* responsible is the goal. One must choose to do both with all your talent and enthusiasm. It is a difficult job for most of us. However, if you understand the difference between success and responsibility, you will cross both finish lines in life's marathon while minimizing stress and maximizing positive feelings both for yourself and those in your care.

CHAPTER TWENTY ONE

SAY HELLO TO YOUR FATHER

Anxiety Management

Anxiety is an essential element of the human survival package as it puts all sensory functions on alert. Unchecked anxiety is a destructive force, both physically and mentally. Rest assured, there is always a light at the end of the tunnel. Sometimes you just have to look hard to find it.

In the spring of 1944 my father received a draft notice for service in the Army. My brother Sammy and I were told that Dad would be leaving soon and that he was going to be a soldier. I had no fear or anxiety about his departure. My maternal grandparents lived next door, my mother said we would pray for him, America would win the war and he would return to us. It all seemed logical.

When the day arrived that he was to report for duty, there was a special dinner at my grandparents' home. It was a happy event. My father was the center of attention. All went well until my grandmother said her goodbye. She held Dad's head gently in her hands, looked deeply into his eyes and spoke to him softly in Italian. She began to weep as she stroked his head. My grandfather embraced his son-in-law, kissed his cheek and quietly spoke a few words of instruction to him in Italian. My father nodded his head in agreement to whatever my grandfather said to him.

My grandparents' tender farewell struck an alarming chord in my brain. I can recall a wave of fear engulfing me. I thought if they are so worried about his going away, maybe he was not coming back. My mother, Sammy, and I went to the porch to say our final goodbye. Dad kissed and hugged Sammy, but he was too young to understand what was happening.

Dad got down on one knee, held my shoulders firmly in his hands, and said directly to me, "Be a big boy and always look after your mother." As he kissed me, I held him firmly around the neck and would not let him loose. He was staying or I was going with him. My grandfather had to literally pry me off of my father. Dad kissed and hugged my mother, turned and went down the steps to the street. I can still recall crying and watching him walk down the street with his suitcase. He would take a few steps, turn around, and look at us with a smile and wave. I expected that he would turn around and come back, but he did not. He could not.

Dad was gone for only two months and returned home unexpectedly. He had been rejected because of a vision problem in his right eye. We were thrilled that he was back. My mother told me much later the rejection hurt him deeply.

That scene of my father's departure came back to me in my adult life when I was about to leave my wife and sons for my first assignment to Vietnam. As my parents had done, I wanted to be certain that Anita and the boys were free from unnecessary anxiety and were assured of my return. It was also important that Anita was settled in a home and had a contingent of friends and family at hand. Life for them was to be as normal as possible. Lastly, it was very important to me to depart with dignity as my father did. Anita and I wanted to manage the natural anxiety of the situation as best we could.

I was finishing up a master's degree program at Cornell University in Ithaca, New York. To finish my course work and prepare for an orderly departure to Vietnam was more than I could handle. The ball, therefore, fell directly into Anita's court. We made a checklist of tasks to be accomplished. She set out to resolve every relocation issue cheerfully and enthusiastically. Anita is a good soldier.

We had planned for Anita and the boys to live near our parents in Johnstown. The lease on a nice house was arranged. Three weeks before my departure the woman who owned the house called to advise us that she did not want to rent to a woman with a husband in Vietnam. She also made it clear that she did not support the war in Vietnam. The house was no longer for rent. She said the lease had been cancelled. We were to call her lawyer if we had questions.

Anita showed no emotion at this news and immediately decided to call an old friend from the 8th Infantry Division who was living in a "Vietnam Waiting Wives" community in Green Cove Springs, Florida. Anita said, "I want to be with my own kind (READ: Army wives) if I cannot be with my family." She called her friend and two days later she had secured a home, sight unseen, in Green Cove Springs.

When we told our parents of the situation, they were irritated and unhappy at our decision to abandon Johnstown and head to Florida. Anita defused the situation quickly by advising them that Army wives are exceptionally resourceful and stable in situations most others would consider stressful. I recall her saying, "We do not fail ourselves or one another; we stick together like glue." After the phone call she said to me, "This was a blessing in disguise. Our parents may feel some anxiety, but I am comfortable with what we have just done." She was not looking back.

Joey was five years old and David was three when we arrived in Green Cove Springs. Our home was small by any standard, but it was well maintained and managed by a kind, competent and caring gentleman. Anita had worked the "Anxiety" list with such dedication that we had only two issues on the list after the movers dropped our goods off at our new home: (1) Sorting out the excess things that would not fit in our house, and (2) Getting Joey into a kindergarten. The former came easier than the latter.

After the sort out, we had goods that required storage and those we decided to donate to a church. Taking on the first issue, Anita called a local moving and storage company in Green Cove Springs and spoke with the manager. She told him our story about the Johnstown lease revoke and our decision to come south. They were at our home the next day, were extremely courteous and even gave Anita a discount on the storage price because I was going "into a combat zone." More than ever she was convinced that she had done the right thing to move to Green Cove Springs. Meanwhile, I attempted to take our giveaway items to the local Catholic Church but discovered it was not a full-time operation.

Intent on giving the items to a church, I pulled out a phone book, closed my eyes and ran my finger down the "church" entry in the Yellow Pages. I stopped at the Orange Avenue Baptist Church.

I telephoned the church. A man answered, identifying himself as "Brother Jim." Everyone had been so kind in Green Cove Springs that I thought that this was most likely some form of a friendly Southern greeting. In Johnstown we called almost everyone "buddy," so I decided to return some of the local goodwill. Picking up on his lead, I said, "Brother Jim, this is Brother Joe." I told him of my pending departure for Vietnam and that we had some items to donate to the church. He said he would be over that afternoon to pick them up in his truck. When he arrived I introduced him to Anita and found he was a very pleasant fellow. After loading the truck and some general conversation, I offered him a glass of sherry. He declined noting that he had to get home for supper. Thanking us for our kindness he drove off into the sunset.

That evening we were talking with our next door neighbor and I told her my "Brother Jim" story. To my horror, she told me that the use of "Brother" was not some Southern euphemism, but was a term of respect in their church. My "Brother Jim" was the pastor of the Orange Avenue Baptist Church. She also told me that Baptists did not drink alcohol and that my offer of sherry was most inappropriate. To sum it up, I was embarrassed at my lack of insight into their denomination and upset that I had treated a man of the cloth so poorly.

Early the next morning I called the church to make an appointment with Brother Jim to apologize for my unintentional but disrespectful behavior. Wearing a suit and tie, I arrived at his office after lunch. He was all smiles and still quite friendly. I explained my ignorance of his beliefs and asked for his forgiveness for offending him. He rose from his chair, put his arm around my shoulder and gently said, "When I saw the Pennsylvania license plates on your car, I knew you were just being friendly. Be assured that I took no offense. In fact, my wife and I had a good laugh over dinner about 'Brother Joe.'"

He then asked if I was prepared for a year in Vietnam and if I was confident that my wife and children were settled in Green Cove Springs. I told him of our intent to manage the anxiety and stress of a year's separation. I reaffirmed that the folks in Green Cove Springs had been so kind to us that their affection for military people was a relief. The only remaining issue was to locate a kindergarten for our son, preferably a Christian one. Anita had called a number of schools and unfortunately all were filled.

He looked at me for a moment seemingly assessing the truthfulness of my words. He then went to his desk, picked up the telephone, and spoke to a woman. He said, "I have a young Army officer in my office who is leaving for Vietnam in three days. He and his wife desire a Christian kindergarten for their five-year old son during his absence. I would like you to put one more seat in the classroom starting next Monday." The person on the other end of the phone obviously gave him a few reasons why she could not do that, but he insisted gently, "Can you not find room for just one more? This is important to me." He listened for a moment and said, "God Bless you," and hung up the phone. He told me that Joey would be enrolled in the school and that, if there was ever anything that my wife required while I was overseas, he would be more than happy to assist. The anxiety of ensuring Joey's education was immediately dissipated. He then turned toward me, put his hands on my shoulders and asked Almighty God to give me prudent courage and return me safely to my wife and children. I left Brother Jim thankful and uplifted by his prayer.

On the day of departure, Anita, the boys and I conducted ourselves with dignity. When I said goodbye to the boys, David made it a point to tell me he would be a good boy for his mother. Joey, being older, realized what was happening and became teary eyed. I held him by his shoulders and said to him, "Joey, I am counting on you to be the man of the house while I am gone. Be sure to look after your mother." He hugged me tightly about the neck, and Anita pulled him away gently when he began to sob. As I walked down the gangway to the plane I looked back every few steps, smiled and burned the picture of them waving goodbye into my mind. I turned just before entering the plane and waved one last time. I wanted to return to them but I couldn't.

I left for Vietnam absent of any useless anxiety about the well-being of my family in that wonderful small Florida town. In our one year of separation, Anita never wrote me one word of bad news and passed on plenty of good news. Some unpleasant things did occur while I was gone but she did not write of those things until they had been resolved. Without anxiety about my family's welfare during my absence, my mind was clear to deal exclusively with my professional responsibilities. She wanted no praise or recognition for her actions during my absence. She was just proud to be an Army wife.

The anxiety of separation was skillfully managed because of Anita's strength of character. Her courage to deal with the situation was communicated to and emulated by the boys. My picture was in their room; we talked on reel-to-reel tapes that were exchanged through the mail. Her love, compassion and insistence on high standards of behavior kept anxiety and depression away from our door. Her pride in being an Army wife, caring for her family and helping others in need, sustained her under conditions less than optimum. I was so proud of Anita and the boys. Their courage permitted me to be all I could be.

In contrast, consider this illustration of unmanaged anxiety's negative effect. When I returned from Vietnam, I flew from Saigon to Seattle and then onward to McGuire Air Force Base in New Jersey. My mother and Aunt Sara arranged a homecoming for me just outside the airbase. Many relatives were present, and they all stayed in adjoining rooms at the same hotel. Knowing my father's aversion to things military, I believed that he would not come to the military terminal on the airbase. When I left the holding area in the terminal, I went into the waiting area searching for my family. It was easy to find my mother and Aunt Sara; they were the ones making the most noise.

After the frenzy of our greeting had passed, my mother took my hand and said, "Joe, say hello to your father." "Is he here?" I asked. Mom said, "He wouldn't miss this moment. He has been under a great deal of anxiety since you left and has experienced so much stress that it has affected his health." She took me to a heavyset man in a brim hat and black topcoat. It was difficult to see the man's face. She said to the man, "Joe, he is back home, he is safe." With that, the collar came down and there was my dad. He had gained at least twenty-five pounds that year and his face and posture looked tired. The man to whom I said goodbye a year earlier had been physically fit and vibrant. This man was old, fatigued, and overweight. I was stunned. I embraced him, and he held me very tight. Not a word was uttered, but when we separated he had tears in his eyes and said, "We are happy to have you back home."

During the party at the hotel, I sat in an overstuffed chair while my dad sat in one next to me, relaxing more every minute. To honor my father, I did not speak of things military but rather, of my rest and recuperation leave in Hawaii with Anita and of the friends I had left behind in Vietnam. I had a flight from Philadelphia to Jacksonville, Florida the next day at 10:00 a.m. but we enjoyed one another's company until well after midnight.

My mother assured me she would wake me in time to catch the flight so I went to bed. The lights were out and I was falling asleep when my father came into the room. He never said a word but kissed my forehead. I said to him, "Dad, I am really happy to be home." He said, "So am I." I quickly fell asleep. When I awoke, I saw that I was not alone; my father had spent the night sleeping in a large chair across from my bed. My mother told me that he told her, "Joe is back home. I want to stay in the room with him tonight to be certain he is okay."

My father's anxiety, depression and stress brought on by my duty in Vietnam were the product of seeing only one side of the coin. He watched too much television and read too many newspapers. My mother told me he internalized every negative TV story and worried needlessly. She said he lived with anxiety every day. He frequently told my mother, "You know that Joe has had the tendency to act then think since he was a child. I hope maturity has suppressed that trait, it could get him killed." When they received a letter from me, he would ask her why I would not speak of what was really happening in the 25th Infantry Division. He had seen the Division in action on the television and was fearful for my safety. The anxiety generated by the negative media reports degraded his health and his outlook on life. She said there was never any good news. While his faith in the Almighty sustained him, he was never the same man after I returned from Vietnam the first time.

When I discussed Dad's health with his close friend John, he agreed that anxiety is a normal and essential human emotion and like so many other issues of the human condition, it must be managed. John explained that my father had done a poor job of managing his anxiety because everyone in the barbershop had a bad story about something they had seen on TV or read about. Dad could never escape the news and he took it all to heart. John noted that uncontrolled anxiety is as destructive as possessing no anxiety. A little anxiety is good; but it must be kept under control.

In my experience, anxiety always seems greatest the first time I encounter a situation. Emotions rooted in the unknown put all my sensory functions on alert. On the other hand, if I have experienced something similar in the past I find it reduces anxiety to manageable levels. Anxiety will destroy your life. You must make the choice to reject anxiety and all its negative companions and focus on the positive by taking charge of your actions and emotions. There is always a light at the end of the tunnel. It's just that sometimes you must persist and be determined to find it.

CHAPTER TWENTY TWO

JOE, HERE IS YOUR NUMBER ONE

Express Your Love and Affection

One's day-to-day work tends to retard expressions of affection and love. It's easy to rationalize that others know and are assured of your love. Until you sincerely express that emotion face to face, the circle of affection is incomplete. Express your appreciation and affection. You will enrich your spirit by sharing this most personal emotion.

My father's death came suddenly and without warning. He told me shortly before he died that he prayed for a quick passing. When I asked him whether he was ill, he told me he thought he was well but had a feeling that his time was getting short. He confided that he wanted to prepare and organize for the event. Accordingly, we spent an evening together discussing my responsibilities in caring for my mother after he was gone. His orders and instructions were both detailed and plentiful. I took notes and clarified his intentions. It was a very business-like discussion. I assured him of my attentive care for Mother's welfare and that his kind words of appreciation and confidence in me were locked in my heart. A heavy note of finality was present in our conversation.

To lighten things up, he jokingly told me he wanted to die on the fifth green at Berkley Hills Golf Course in Johnstown. He had played that hole so well over the years that he thought that would be a good place to pass from this life into the next. Since my father was a spiritual man I was confident that his request for a quick passing would be honored. Unfortunately, I was unprepared for his permanent absence. The day before he died he played golf and took my mother to dinner at one of his favorite restaurants. Returning home, they played Scrabble for a while and then went to bed. He awoke during the night not feeling well. My mother, thinking it was an upset stomach, advised him to drink some Brioski (an Italian Alka-Seltzer) and he would feel better.

At six o'clock in the morning he called my mother and calmly told her that he thought that he had just had a heart attack. My mother, frightened, called the ambulance service to take him to the hospital. He was reportedly at peace with himself and the situation. The hospital subjected him to a series of tests. There were no indications of any irregularity. It was decided that he should stay in the hospital overnight for observation.

My mother was with him during the day and was offered an evening meal with the hospital nuns who lived nearby. After dining, she came back to my Dad's hospital room. They spoke for a while. He told her she should go home as he was fine and would be released the next day. My Uncle Carmel would take her home.

Mother told me that they then exchanged some tender words. She leaned over the bed and held him in her arms. She kissed him on the cheek and, just for an instant, thought that he had stopped breathing. Before she could move, Mom said, she felt him tense up for just a moment while she was still holding him. Then he relaxed; he never said a word. When she turned and looked at the heart monitor, it showed no heartbeat. It was a straight line. The nurse attempted to bring him back but he was gone to God, exactly as he had asked. He was sixty-nine years old.

Anita and I had not known that he was in the hospital. My parents thought it was a minor affair and did not want to upset us. When he died, my mother called Anita and told her of my father's passing. Anita loved my father dearly. They were a mutual admiration society. It was a family joke that she was called Saint Anita because she had to live with me. My father often quipped that he loved her more than he loved me.

I was working in the Pentagon that evening when Anita called in tears. After she told me my father had died, I was overcome with an instant flood of grief. Dear General Benjamin Register stopped what he was doing, took me to his home at Fort Myer, and let me get some of the sadness out of my soul. What a kind man to tolerate my tears and listen to my incoherent ramblings. Collecting my emotions, I went home and Anita and I left for Johnstown early the next day.

The next few days are still a blur. One person after another passing by my father's casket told us stories about his integrity, friendship, dependability, loyalty, moral strength in the face of adversity, and stories of his concern for the welfare of others. It was a celebration of his character. He was a man who did not fail others.

We acquired an extra room at the funeral home just to accommodate the number of people coming to see my father for the last time. For two days there was a steady stream of friends waiting to pay their last respects. At one point the line was thirty minutes long, but the kind folks waited.

Many tears were shed and I was emotionally exhausted on the day of his Funeral Mass. Before his casket was closed, my brothers and sister and I said our last earthly words to our dear father. My mother introduced each one of us to him as if he were alive. My youngest brother Michael went first, then my sister Dolly, Sammy and finally, me. While I stood at the casket with my weeping mother at my arm, she said to my father, "Joe, here is your Number One." My father was a movie fan of the Chinese detective, Charlie Chan. Charlie referred to his sons by their number in birth order. Since I was the eldest, in his lighter moments, Dad called me "Number One Son." My mother told me he often used that term of affection for me when they were alone and discussing their children.

The emotion of the moment was extraordinary. I held his hand for the last time and could not speak. I never seized the opportunity to tell him how much I cared for him and how I appreciated his care and concern for me. Words always seemed inadequate for the task. I regret that omission deeply.

Friends reassured me that my father had lived his life with a strong moral character held to a high standard. They noted that the many people who came to bid him farewell were actually acknowledging their affection and esteem for the way he lived his life. It was an honor to have a father who was so well respected by so many very good men and women.

Flowers were in profusion at the funeral home. Their gentle sweet aroma induced a feeling of life overcoming death in that room. Relatives from all over the East Coast came to be with us. It was the last time we would all be together.

Lying in bed that night I recalled that the respect shown to my father was earned by his many charitable and compassionate deeds for family, friends, and even strangers. This was not to be a time of sadness but a time of joy for all that he had accomplished in his life. My father had touched many lives in a positive fashion. I made the choice then and there that I wanted to go to the next life as he did; respected, loved, and prepared for the event. More than anything, I vowed that before my mother passed to the next world, I would not permit her to go without expressing my deep love and appreciation for her loving maternal stewardship. I carried out that vow before she died and it has brought me peace.

A moral character coupled with a responsible concern for one's fellow man carries with it a sense of tranquil, almost imperceptible, virtue while an individual is alive. When one passes to the next life, that sense of peaceful, moral excellence does not die. Rather, it is suddenly and conspicuously revealed to all those they touched while they were here. It is the last act of the Passing of Wisdom.

It is important for us to make the choice to express our feelings for those we love while we still have the chance. This is a choice you must seize.

Epilogue

America Through Foreign Eyes

After six months in the Army I began to better understand the wisdom of my parents' game plan for my life. The Army's gold standard for performance was based on character, talent and experience. Highly talented lieutenants with demonstrated character deficiencies were summarily dismissed from the inventory of those who were to be considered for advancement. I was shocked when I saw a lieutenant I considered a role model soldier dismissed because of two incidents of letters of indebtedness.

Within my first year of service to our Republic, my military mentors confirmed the strong and positive relationship between character and performance. Accordingly, over my next 36 years of military and public service I did my utmost to live up to the high personal and professional standards of the Army. I also did my best to instill those high standards in those who served with me. The Officer's Performance Report measured and recorded the individual's achievement in meeting those elevated standards and was a profile of the individual's potential.

Notably, I have written thousands of performance reports during my 36+ years of public service. In the early 1990s, an allied officer I had met when we were much younger had attained a high rank in his country's military. We reconnected while I was assigned as the Chief of Staff at NATO's Allied Forces Southern Europe Headquarters. My friend was well educated, had a previous assignment in the United States and spoke English flawlessly. When I took the Chief of Staff job in Naples, Italy he sent me a nice note of congratulations and requested that I forward a copy of all performance reports on his nation's officers directly to him. This was not unusual as other countries requested the same procedure.

After a few months a report was due on one of his officers. The man was highly talented and of significant potential but I was compelled to report that the officer occasionally had difficulty in speaking truthfully. Visiting my friend in his country shortly thereafter, I learned that one of the issues on the list of "Topics to Be Discussed Privately" was "Performance Reports."

When we were alone in his office my friend told me with a smile that my evaluation of his officers was uniquely American. He referred to the officer I had highlighted as being loose with the truth and said, "This is the officer's first assignment abroad and he requires some coaching. You see, in my country it is our culture not to tell the truth when we feel that a question has been asked that is no business of the questioner or others who may be listening. Rather than be rude and not answer the question, it is more appropriate that some answer other than the truth is rendered.

"We all do it and we understand the other person is not telling the truth. It is our culture as we are a very politically sensitive society. If someone does not tell the truth, we know there is a good reason for that response and we do not press the issue. We simply try another way to find the answer. We can do this because we are a relatively small and homogeneous population and everyone knows the rules."

Noting that while the officer's conduct would be tolerated at home, my friend said it was inappropriate for international service. He asked me to call him directly if the officer in question did not modify his behavior in the immediate future. I assured him I would comply with his request.

We had a private dinner together later that evening and he told me the following story. "When I went to the United States for the first time, I spent two weeks in New York City at our United Nations Embassy for an orientation. I was shocked at what I saw. The streets were packed with Europeans of all nationalities, Africans, Asians, and Latin Americans. Most were in a hurry to get somewhere yet all seemed courteous and most importantly, they seemed happy. They were walking the streets without animosity or interference from one another. I could see little presence of government as I walked some distance without seeing a policeman. It was very noisy; men who were highly dressed stood obediently in line at a sausage cart with beggars to buy a sandwich. However, men and women crossed the street imprudently when the pedestrian sign told them to stay on the sidewalk; it was a clear act of disobedience. After a few weeks I realized that this was the nature of America. People were free to go about their lives as long as they stayed within the wide boundaries of laws subject to broad interpretation."

He continued, "A little later, from my office in Washington, DC I was taken to Baltimore on a weekend to observe an Italian Festival. While it was advertised as an Italian festival, I was surprised to find that almost no one at the festival spoke Italian. In fact, the best pizza we ate was made by a Greek. It seemed that everyone was celebrating being Italian when in fact, there were more non-Italians in attendance than those of Italian heritage. One American of African descent was wearing a T-shirt that said, 'Kiss me, I'm Italian.' To my amazement, women were kissing the man and everyone was laughing and joking. I asked one man selling sausage if he were Italian. He said, 'No, not me, my grandparents were Italian. I'm an American.' People were singing, eating and drinking with abandon; they were very loud. I could not find a policeman in the crowd. On the way home I saw two policemen at the parking garage entrance and they were socializing with the crowd and eating pizza. Looking back, I think non-American national cultures are celebrated for their art, food, music and the like but the people enjoying the celebration were Americans first and foremost.

"It took me a full three years to have some understanding of the Americans. I have come to believe that Americans do not care about a person's religion, race or ancestors, as long as they adopt the model American character which abides by the rule of law and that they show respect for one another. Hope for a better future based on persistence and personal determination seems to be an underlying tenet of American life. In America, individuals have many choices concerning their lives and future. There are far fewer life choice opportunities available to individuals in my country and life is much simpler; that is, barbers' children become barbers, not Army generals. In America, the issue is not whether an individual has choices but rather, what choices do they make. I believe that the quality of life of most Americans is a function of the choices they make and those choices are defined by their character. Being an American has more to do with personal character and much less with a person's group identity. Actually, I believe the American national character is the centerpiece of your culture. Character focuses on the individual, not the individual's race, religion or ethnic group, and America is all about the individual."

Then he turned to me and said, "General Laposata, you are living proof of my theory. Your grandparents were Italian, they came to America 80 years ago and they embraced the American language and character to build a better life for their children and grandchildren. You have been given America's full trust and confidence to serve as a lieutenant general because you reflect the national culture. The only thing Italian about you is your name. In my country your family would have to fill the graveyard with generations of bodies before we would even consider you trustworthy of an officer's commission. You chose the Army as a career, applied the full measure of your talent and character to the task and were rewarded for your effort. It is improbable that would happen in my country as your family has no history or connections.

"I am a subject of my nation and I love it dearly despite its inward-looking and highly conservative nature. I would give my life for its well-being. America will always surprise and amaze me because your national character is very flexible and responsive to all manner of situations. Americans are not restricted by prejudices and traditions that entrap the rest of the world. Opportunities are available to all citizens. Be assured that the character of your nation is an aggregate of the character of its citizens.

"Keep inspiring your children because the quality of character resident in the average citizen will determine the destiny of your nation. Perhaps America's example will inspire the rest of the world to live together on a higher level. With a high American military presence in Europe since 1945, we have experienced the longest period of peace and prosperity on the continent since the Middle Ages. The presence of an American military culture and peace in Europe is not a coincidence."

It was late. I retired to my room in the government hotel and wrote the above so that I would never forget this man's insights about my beloved America. He was one of those rare outsiders who saw America for what it was more clearly than those of us who live here.

I recently found my notes of the above encounter that took place in 1992 and was motivated by my friend's thoughts about inspiring the American character in our children. In that regard, I am hopeful that the preceding stories have informed, enlightened and perhaps even entertained so that we may, each in our own way, inspire our children to become productive and determined citizens persistently working toward a better future for themselves and our nation. Sooner than later our children will find they must bear the responsibility to support and defend our precious Constitution, the grantor of all our liberties. That effort will require every ounce of their character, talent and experience. They must make the proper choices to insure they are prepared for the challenge. God bless them... The preservation of our Constitution is a sacred trust.